500 Things You Didn't Know About Stranger Things

Nick Stones

Contents

PREFACE

Do you want more arcane Stranger Things trivia than you can shake at a Demogorgon at? Well, you've come to the right place. The following volume contains all manner of trivia relating to the blockbuster Netflix show. There are facts, among many other topics way too numerous to mention, about the origins of the show, the cast, special effects, monsters, Dungeons & Dragons, guns & weapons, Vecna, the Mind Flayer, episodes, Easter eggs, and pop culture influences in both film and literature.

I have avoided anything TOO obvious (you don't really need to be told, for example, that Stranger Things is a bit like Stephen King's The Mist or that it homages Spielberg's E.T. the Extra-Terrestrial umpteen times in the first season - you already KNOW this sort of stuff) and planted my focus more on the sort of stuff that you might not know - as opposed to the obvious. One thing I've mostly avoided here too is anachronisms or goofs - where a food product or song which is too contemporary for the 1980s is erroneously included in an episode. This sort of stuff is quite interesting and can be fun but it would be a bit tedious to endlessly list all the anachronisms in the show.

Much of the material in this book comes my own personal fandom of Stranger Things and things I've noticed while watching the show but I am also indebted to some invaluable research sources. The must buy Telos Publishing book Upside Down: The Unofficial and Unauthorised Stranger Things Companion (which is by far the best Stranger Things book available if you ask me) by James Forster and also the fun 1000 Facts About Stranger Things by Nick Bryce were both handy reference points - as too was the Stranger Things Wiki.

500 THINGS YOU DIDN'T KNOW ABOUT STRANGER THINGS

(1) Vecna's lair (which is officially known as his Mindscape) and Henry Creel's first wander through the terrifying (not that Henry finds it terrifying - he seems to love the place!) Upside Down was partly inspired by some of the bleaker work of the German painter Caspar David Friedrich. Friedrich, who died in 1840, was known for depicting solitary figures in lonely landscapes.

(2) Finn Wolfhard said that when he had to kiss Millie Bobby Brown in the season one finale The Upside Down he sort of accidentally head-butted her. He thinks this is why she famously didn't seem to enjoy the kiss very much at the time!

(3) In Stranger Things 4, Eleven has to go into a sensory deprivation tank in the missile silo in order to retrieve her memories and hopefully get her powers back. Millie Bobby Brown said she had a couple of intense days during the production of season four where she spent up to ten hours a day in the tank and suffered from acute claustrophobia as a consequence. The water had loads of salt so she could float easily and they had to use a large overhead microphone to relay instructions because it was very difficult for her to hear anything - what with her ears often being underwater!

(4) In order to get the likeness for the little 1979 version of Eleven in Stranger Things 4, the special effects department used clips from Once Upon a Time in Wonderland - a television show which Millie Bobby Brown appeared in when she was nine years-old - as a reference.

(5) Stranger Things was loosely inspired by Camp Hero at Montauk - which is obviously why the show was originally going to have this title. Montauk is a village on the tip of Long Island. There is an old decommissioned military base there called Camp Hero which was one of the SAGE radar stations of Air Defense Command. The main purpose of these stations was to warn of any threat of nuclear attack. The base at Camp Hero, though apparently abandoned now, is still fenced off and guarded. The imposing Cold War radar still stands -

silent and motionless. A number of conspiracies have been floated in relation to the base. There are stories that the government secretly buried a nuclear reactor there and it is often alleged to have been part of the secret MK-Ultra project (which was basically a clandestine experiment by the CIA to see if mind control and remote viewing was actually real). In 1992, Preston B. Nichols (along with Peter Moon) wrote a book called The Montauk Project: Experiments in Time in which Nichols claimed that after discovering he was a 'telepath' he had visited Montauk - where the caretaker of the old military base seemed to know who he was. Nichols claims that he was once in charge of a secret project at Camp Hero which opened a rip in time and made him experience alternate realities. That was merely the tip of the iceberg as Camp Hero was also allegedly subject to aliens, monsters, and time travel.

The Montauk Project: Experiments in Time rather gives the game away in the introduction when it invites us to read the book that follows as a work of fiction should we choose. No one in their right mind believed that this book had any basis in reality. Nonetheless, the conspiracy theories related to Camp Hero tickled the imaginations of the Duffers and made them want to set the show in Montauk. In the original pilot script for the show Jim Hopper lives in a shack on the beach and the Byers house is right next to Camp Hero. While the general story and concepts in the show remained the same it did have a very different atmosphere and aura by moving the action from Long Island to Indiana. In the original early concept for the show, when it was still called Montauk, there were even plans to have everything take place in a blanket of heavy snow. A sort of Stranger Things meets 30 Days of Night.

(6) The 1979 version of Eleven makes a 'superhero landing' (head down, one knee, arms apart) in The Massacre at Hawkins Lab after vanquishing Henry Creel at the lab. This is a nice payoff given Eleven's depression earlier in the season at the loss of her powers. She's finally a superhero once again. The 'superhero landing' (which is mocked in the film Deadpool) is associated with characters like Black Widow in the Marvel movies but goes way back. Iron Man has been depicted with his own unique 'landing' in the comics for decades. You can see examples of the superhero landing in Japanese anime, The Matrix trilogy, and the Blade movies with Wesley Snipes

- which all obviously predate the MCU.

(7) The casting in Stranger Things was quite lucky in that the stars seemed to align in allowing the Duffer Brothers to get the perfect people for these roles - regardless of how famous they were or how much acting experience they did or didn't have. Joe Keery was working as a waiter when he auditioned for the show while Shannon Purser had never done any professional acting and was still at school and working part-time in a cinema. Millie Bobby Brown's family had moved back to England and she had become disillusioned with acting after a series of failed auditions. She was then told about Montauk (to become Stranger Things) and reluctantly taped an audition in an American accent. Caleb McLaughlin, who had worked primarily on the stage as a child actor, was also bruised by a number of failed auditions and very nearly didn't bother to go to the Montauk auditions. Finn Wolfhard, like Millie Bobby Brown, sent in a taped audition (from his home in Canada).

Finn was only available because of a change of director on the (Stephen King) IT movie. He had to wait to see if the new director still wanted him for the part of Richie Tozier. If there hadn't been a change of director and delay on IT then Finn Wolfhard wouldn't have been in Stranger Things. Winona Ryder was the first person targeted by the show but they had no idea if she would be interested or even return their phone calls. The hiring of Winona Ryder was a great coup for the show because it meant they had a genuine star name to headline the project. This meant that they could cast whoever they wanted in the other parts - even if they were not big names. Charlie Heaton was a former rock band drummer with little acting experience when he auditioned for Montauk. He did a video cam audition and then completely forgot about it. Months later he was woken up in bed in England at 4 in the morning by the Duffers on the telephone telling him he had the part of Jonathan Byers.

Gaten Matarazzo was a Broadway kid who hadn't done much screen acting but Shawn Levy and the Duffers decided he had to be in the show as soon as they met him. Gaten's cleidocranial dysplasia (a condition which meant he didn't have any teeth) made Gaten's agent fear he wouldn't secure any acting work but Stranger Things happily proved this fear was unfounded. Noah Schnapp thought he had messed up his audition because he had a headache that day. He put it out of mind and forget about it. He was at summer camp when the Duffers telephoned to say he had the part of Will Byers. It would probably be stretching things to say that David Harbour was an unknown actor at the time of his casting as Hopper for he was an experienced actor with many credits but he definitely wasn't a leading man until the Duffers came along. The Duffers decided to cast Harbour as Hopper after watching him in a television show called Manhattan - which was about the development of the first atomic bomb. Harbour played a scientist named Dr Reed Akley in Manhattan. Had any network been casting Stranger Things they would in all probability have gone for a bigger name as Hopper (even the pitch booklet for Montauk by the Duffers suggested Sam Rockwell was the sort of name who could play Hopper) than David Harbour. The hunch by the Duffers that Harbour was perfect for Hopper turned out to be right though as you couldn't really imagine anyone else in the part now.

(8) While he was in the makeup chair being transformed into Vecna on the set of Stranger Things 4, Jamie Campbell Bower would play some thrash metal tunes to help him get into character. Ironically, another song he listened to a lot was Placebo's cover of Running Up That hill.

(9) As any Stranger Things fan worth their salt will already know, the show was originally going to be called Montauk and set by the coast. When these plans were abandoned they had to come up with a brand new title. The titles they considered were The Rift, The Nether, Sentinel, Flickers, The Keep, The Tesseract, and Wormhole. The Keep was the title of a weird by cultish Michael Mann horror film and The Tesseract was the title of an Alex Garland novel so no prizes for originality of those two fronts (which probably explains why they were not chosen). A title they nearly settled on was Indigo but Matt Duffer eventually came up with Stranger Things - which was inspired by the Stephen King story Needful Things. Ross Duffer and lead actor David Harbour did not like Stranger Things as the new title at all and made their feelings known. However, no one could think of anything better so Stranger Things became the new name of the show.

(10) The United States Department of Energy is not in reality, you won't be surprised to learn, involved in the development of super powered children in real life. The Department of Energy was created in 1977 and is involved in energy research and production. This department is heavily involved in the United States nuclear program and has many facilities and laboratories around the country. Because these facilities - for obvious reasons of national security - are sometimes rather secretive (even mysterious) this gave the Duffer Brothers enough wriggle room to depict the fictitious Hawkins Department of Energy as a sinister place led by a man (Brenner) with a questionable sense of ethics.

The Hawkins Department of Energy exteriors you see in the show are the former Georgia Mental Health Institute - which operated as a psychiatric hospital from 1965 to 1997. The hospital and its campus were then purchased by Emory University with the intention of turning this building and land into a biotech hub. When these plans were abandoned this allowed the Stranger Things production team to use the building for their foreboding exterior shots of the lab. There are now plans to demolish the building and build an old people's home on the site. Patrick Henry High School, a defunct school building in located in Stockbridge, Georgia, which doubles for the Hawkins schools in the show, is also due for demolition to make way for a new school to be built on the site. It seems that many of the most famous Stranger Things 'landmarks' may not exist for much longer so visit them and get a photograph while you still can!

(11) When they shot the scene in episode eight of season two where Dustin explains that the Flayer has an urge to conquer and considers itself superior and Steve replies by saying "Like the Germans", Charlie Heaton laughed so much that he had to leave the set so they could finish the scene.

(12) When his sequel Avatar - The Way of Water came out, James Cameron talked about future Avatar sequels and commented that footage of the younger actors in the franchise was already in the can for use in later installments to avoid what he called the 'Stranger Things effect' of actors being preposterously older than the characters they are playing. While one could understand the general point he was making (one thinks of Walt in the TV show Lost -

where the child actor Malcolm David Kelley had to be written out of
the show because he hit puberty and was patently aging too quickly
for the timeline of the story), Cameron's specific reference to
Stranger Things made no sense whatsoever. Millie Bobby Brown
was only 17 when she made Stranger Things 4. It's not as if she was
a 33 year-old pretending to be a high schooler. Noah Schnapp was
even younger than Millie. Stranger Things does also incorporate a
time jump between each season. It isn't as if all the seasons take
place in the same week.

(13) The body double for the young 1979 lab version of Eleven in
Stranger Things 4 was child actor Martie Blair. Blair was best
known for playing Bella in the soap opera The Young and the
Restless. She even shaved her hair to play the young Eleven in
Stranger Things 4. CGI was used to impose the likeness of a younger
Millie Bobby Brown over Blair's face. Although Martie Blair sort of
resembles a nine year-old version of Millie Bobby Brown they
decided this would be the most realistic thing to do. Blair worked a
lot with Millie Bobby Brown on the set in order to mimic Millie's
body language and movements as Eleven. The results were certainly
impressive - aside from one slightly awkward shot where the young
Eleven is looking up at Henry Creel. During post-production Millie
had to use something called the Lola machine to copy Martie's
movements so that her likeness could be imposed.

(14) In the original plan for Stranger Things 2, Eleven was going to
'mercy kill' her catatonic mother Teresa 'Terry' Ives. Upon reflection
though the writers decided this might be rather too dark and so
excised this detail from the scripts.

(15) The average length of a Stranger Things episode is 61 minutes.
This is mostly due to season four - which had an average episode
length of 86 minutes. That was considerably longer than than the
previous three seasons. There is no standard length for an episode of
the show. They can run for however long the Duffer Brothers decide.

(16) The highest rated episode of Stranger Things on IMDB is The
Massacre at Hawkins Lab with 9.6. This is certainly not a bad shout
at all as The Massacre at Hawkins Lab is a spectacular episode and
deserving of the highest praise. Stranger Things 4 actually bucks a

trend on IMDB because in all the previous three seasons the finale was always the highest rated episode on the site. That isn't the case with season four - where the finale The Piggyback only ranks third after The Massacre at Hawkins Lab and Dear Billy.

(17) Millie Bobby Brown thinks that when it comes to Eleven and Dr Brenner, Eleven developed a serious case of Stockholm Syndrome. Stockholm syndrome is a condition in which hostages develop a psychological bond with their captors.

(18) By far the least popular arc of season four with fans was Hopper's incarceration in a Russian prison. This was not helped by the fact that he spent the ENTIRE season there. Hopper actually escaped twice but still kept going back to the prison! While there was some sterling acting by David Harbour and an exciting climax to the Russian portion of season four, it remains the fact that you don't tune into Stranger Things to watch a prison drama. There are plenty of other places you can get that.

(19) You may have noticed that Keith, who was the Palace Arcade manager in season two and the hiring boss at Family Video at the end of season three, was completely absent from Stranger Things 4. This was because Matty Cardarople, who plays Keith in the show, suffered a stroke in real life and needed some time to recover. Matty is apparently doing better now and has hopes that Keith might make an appearance in Stranger Things 5.

(20) By 1985 there were about 12,000 video stores in the United States. Steve and Robin would certainly have had no shortage of customers at Family Video in Hawkins.

(21) The production of the first season of Stranger Things was incredibly low-key in hindsight. There was practically no coverage when it began shooting and hardly any promotion when it was due to be released. Many members of the cast presumed the show would fly under the radar and quickly be forgotten (which would obviously have kiboshed any hope of a second season). In a sense then one can see how shrewd Netflix executives were in their approach. They were confident that the show was good and would have a lot of mainstream appeal so they worked on the basis that good word of

mouth would propel the show to success. In the end this is exactly what happened. Netflix were so confident in the show that they secretly asked the Duffers to begin writing season two before season season one had even come out. This confidence all proved more than justified.

(22) Matt and Ross Duffer said that after the success of season one in 2016 they wrote down every idea they could think of in relation to what could happen in the show and where it might go. There were so many ideas that they couldn't possibly use all of them in Stranger Things 2 so what they did was 'bank' the unused ideas and put them on ice for possible use in the future. Some of the unused concepts in Stranger Things 2 will actually form the basis of Stranger Things 5 - the fifth and final season of the show. This was an object lesson in how to play the creative long game!

(23) David Harbour was appearing in a play called Mad House in London's West End when the second volume of season four dropped on Netflix. Harbour said at the time he hoped that a lot of people would come out to see 'Hopper' in the flesh and then get into the play and forget all about Stranger Things.

(24) Stranger Things merch has, not surprisingly, exploded with the immense popularity of the show around the world. What is though the most valuable Stranger Things item on the market? Well, it appears to be a Hopper Gold Funko autographed by David Harbour. This is valued at $6,500.

(25) David Harbour lost eighty pounds to play Hopper in season four. He did this with Pilates and occasional fasting. Pilates is a form of exercise that focuses on balance, posture, strength and flexibility. Harbour said the weight loss isn't something he plans to do again in a hurry and that he eventually put most of the weight back on. It was certainly a far cry from Stranger Things 3 - where Harbour deliberately put weight on to make Hopper seem slobby and someone who was indulging in too much comfort eating.

(26) Matthew Modine said that when he was given the part of Dr Brenner he found that the character had an awful lot of expositional dialogue. He asked that this dialogue be given to other characters in

Brenner's scenes so that Brenner could come across as a man of few words - which made him more mysterious.

(27) David Harbour, as you probably know, is married to the British singer Lily Allen. They didn't meet at some swanky celebrity function though. Oh no. They actually met on the ultra-exclusive dating app Raya.

(28) The exterior used for the Byers house in the early seasons was a real house at 149 Coastline Road in Fayetteville, Georgia. In 2022 this house was put up for sale for $300,000 and sold in one week. One buyer bid $600,000 so it went for well above the asking price. The house will reportedly be turned into an Airbnb. It was estimated that it would cost $100,000 to make the three bedroom house modern and ship shape.

(29) Gaten Matarazzo said it only really dawned on him that Stranger Things was a big deal and he was now famous when he saw a Lego version of his character Dustin Henderson.

(30) Finn Wolfhard had a bone to pick with the bike Mike Wheeler had to ride in season one. Finn said the gears didn't work and it was like trying to pedal a tank. As a consequence of this Finn did not enjoy the cycling scenes featuring the kids because they left him feeling as if he had just run a marathon. He was doubly unlucky on season one because the kids rode their bikes a lot.

(31) If anyone stole Stranger Things 4 from under the noses of the regular cast (though the regular cast were pretty amazing themselves) it was Joseph Quinn as Eddie Munson. When they were casting this role, for the auditions the Duffers made the would be Eddie Munsons do the scene where we first meet Eddie in the school canteen. Now, this is not an easy scene to do because there is a lot of dialogue and Eddie has to be quite manic and slightly crazed but also veer on the right side of likeable. A tricky balancing act you might say. He also has to be charismatic too. There were then a lot of boxes to tick and hoops to jump through for any actor performing this challenging audition. According to the Duffers this audition scene certainly separated the wheat from the chaff and it was Joseph Quinn who rose to the top of the pile by performing it with gusto and

perfect timing. They knew right away they had their Eddie Munson and Quinn's performance in season four more than validated this decision.

(32) Argyle's trusty pizza van in season four is a 1984 Volkswagen Vanagon.

(33) Chase Stokes, star of the Netflix show Outer Banks, said he auditioned to play Steve Harrington in Stranger Things but messed up his audition by forgetting most of his lines. Banks did still appear in the show though - if only briefly. He played a student named Reed in the season one episode The Monster.

(34) Hopper's firearm in seasons one and three is a Smith & Wesson Model 66. This gun was used by Sheriff Will Teasle in First Blood. It was also used by Sheriff Pope in Wayward Pines - a show that the Duffers worked on early in their career.

(35) The character with the most lines in a season four episode is Dustin Henderson with 55 in The Massacre at Hawkins Lab.

(36) The Morten Harket quiff sported by Steve Harrington in season one was expressly designed to make him visually annoying. Steve is outrageously self-absorbed and arrogant in much of season one and his pompadour hairstyle is all you need to know about his character. This is clearly a kid who spends an awful lot of his time gazing adoringly into the mirror. The construction of Steve as the irritating and often obnoxious teen villain of season one was masterful in hindsight. Not only did it serve to make Jonathan punching him in the alley one of the most cathartic moments in the history of the show but it also made the rehabilitation of Steve in the back end of season one more surprising and more effective. Steve's remarkable hair survived beyond season one but it became part of his new action hero status. Steve Harrington's hair was officially no longer annoying.

(37) Due to Covid restrictions - and doubtless time and expense - Dacre Montgomery shot his nightmare flashback cameo as Billy Hargrove in Stranger Things 4 in Australia and then it was spliced in with the episode Dear Billy. Despite his lack of interaction with the

cast, Montgomery's usual intensity is plain to see and he more than makes the most of his chance to play Billy again.

(38) Kate Bush famously has an important sonic role in Stranger Things 4 as the musical guardian of Max Mayfield. When the producers decided that they wanted to use her song Running Up That Hill in the show they had to, as is custom, approach the artist to ask permission. Given that Kate Bush is rather reclusive and enigmatic and not known for wildly embracing the mainstream of popular culture (she once turned down an offer to sing the theme song for the Bond film Moonraker) it was certainly open to question whether or not contact would be made - let alone permission to use Running Up That Hill. To the delight of the Duffer Brothers though it transpired that Kate Bush was actually a big fan of Stranger Things and more than happy to let her song be used in the show. This though is not necessarily the rule but rather the exception. The Stranger Things producer and director Shawn Levy has said that they do get a surprising amount of rejections when they request permission to use famous songs.

(39) The diorama of Hopper's cabin that Eleven takes to school at the start of season four is in a box for Reebok sneakers.

(40) The film mentioned the most when the Duffers talk about the influences of Stranger Things is the 1987 Clive Barker film Hellraiser. In this film an ordinary house hides a dark secret. A man named Frank is secretly lurking the attic. He solved a puzzle box called the Lament Configuration and opened a doorway to another dimension - which looked an awful lot like Hell. Demonic figures known as Cenobites emerged and killed Frank in a most grisly fashion. Or did they? Frank is resurrected by blood but in order to fully repair his body he's going to need an awful lot more. It isn't just the dimensional angle to Hellraiser which connects it to Stranger Things but also the special effects. Hellraiser was made in the last era of practical effects and this movie is what inspired the Duffers to go for a 50/50 split on practical/digital effects in season one (which definitely wouldn't be the case on later seasons). In season four Vecna owes quite a bit to Pinhead - the chief villain of the Hellraiser franchise. Pinhead, like Vecna, is not a manic crazed monosyllabic horror monster. He's articulate and calm.

(41) Jamie Campbell Bower needed 25 pieces of latex and silicone rubber glued to his body to transform into Vecna. The reason they wanted an actor in a suit for Vecna is that they wanted to go back to the DNA of season one where the Demogorgon was mostly Mark Steger in an elaborate monster suit. The fact that Bower was on the set as Vecna interacting with the actors was a great advantage because if Vecna had been a special effect then the cast would have had to react to a tennis ball on a piece of string or something and Vecna would have been added in months later as a digital effect.

(42) Eggo waffles were invented in San Jose, California, by three brothers, Tony, Sam, and Frank Dorsa. They also had their own brand of mayonnaise and potato chips. There was even an Eggos restaurant in Redondo Beach at one point. In 1953, the Dorsa brothers, after perfecting a method of cooking and freezing waffles, introduced Eggo frozen waffles to supermarkets throughout the United States. The Eggo brand was purchased by Kellogs in 1968. Does Millie Bobby Brown like eggo waffles? This is a question that has long occupied the minds of the greatest academics in the world. Millie has, for her art, been nibbling on waffles since 2015 on Stranger Things sets. Season one saw the most waffle action for Millie as Mike Wheeler often smuggled them down into the basement for Eleven when she was a little fugitive on the run from Brenner's sinister lab.

On her press junket for Enola Holmes 2, Millie was asked if she really liked eggo waffles and gave a firm no. She doesn't like eggo waffles and uses a spit bucket if she has to eat them in the show. Millie enjoys carrots, cheese, avocados, salads, and various foods but eggo waffles will not be found in her grocery basket.

(43) It was alleged in 2022 that Netflix had started editing some of the old episodes of the show and changing things. A specific scene mentioned was in season one where Jonathan is lurking around outside the Harrington house taking photographs. It was alleged that this scene had been edited to make Jonathan look like less of a lurking 'peeper' than he appeared in the scene. In response the Stranger Things social media said this story was not true. No old episodes had been edited and they never would be. They also argued that fans were remembering the Jonathan scene all wrong and that he

wasn't there trying to take photographs of Nancy and Steve.

(44) There is no clear official consensus on the best or worst season
of Stranger Things because these things are naturally subjective. The
critic ratings on Rotten Tomatoes rank the seasons in order with
season one the highest rated and season four the lowest. This would
appear to be a contradiction to the general view that Stranger Things
4 was a return to form and an improvement over season three. The
audience ratings on RT are more or less the same pattern as the critic
ratings - though with seasons three and four tied for last. Stranger
Things 4 could possibly be a victim of the fact there are simply more
reviews - which make it more vulnerable to the sniffy critic
determined to nitpick the show and be a party pooper. IMDB, by
contrast, has higher ratings for the season four episodes as a whole
than the season three ones - which feels about right. Stranger Things
3 was highly entertaining but it did feel like the most generic season
of the show with the lack of lab intrigue and wholesale mining of
Invasion of the Body Snatchers for its plot. Stranger Things 4 felt
much grander and more lavish than season three and episodes like
Dear Billy and The Massacre at Hawkins Lab were the show firing
on all cylinders.

At the time of its release there were some complaints that season two
was a rehash of season one but this always felt very unfair (season
two has some new characters and separates Eleven from the other
children - it is plainly not merely giving you the exact same thing
again) and time has been kind to season two in that its IMDB ratings,
The Lost Sister aside, are very strong. In so far as a consensus does
exist it would appear that season one is generally considered to be
the best season of the show - and this seems perfectly valid as season
one was very charming and also had the element of surprise in that
Stranger Things was not hyped or heavily promoted. The seasons
that followed arrived with much more expectation. The quality of the
show has generally been very consistent and impressive through the
course of its duration. You may favour one season over another but
it is fair to say that Stranger Things has never been anything other
than a very entertaining show with high production values and a
talented ensemble cast.

(45) The Duffer Brothers got an awful lot of rejections when they

first tried to pitch Stranger Things to television and streaming companies. All told, they estimate that over a dozen people turned them down before a deal was struck with Netflix. There were a number of factors in why Stranger Things was so difficult to sell. The first problem was the fact that the Duffers were barely known and had little to no clout in Hollywood. They had previously made a horror film called Hidden which sat in mothballs for two years and was then a financial disaster when it got a limited release. They had also worked as writers on the first season of the television show Wayward Pines. While the first season of that show was watchable enough it was hardly the sort of thing to launch writers into superstardom. The second problem the Duffers faced was that Stranger Things would plainly be riffing on Stephen King a lot and Stephen King adaptations are famously hit or miss on television. Take that terrible television series based on Under the Dome for evidence.

The third stumbling block for the Duffers was that they wanted a gang of kids to be the main characters in their show and the television and streaming executives they spoke to thought this was a stupid idea doomed to failure. They thought the Duffers should get rid of the kids and just keep Hopper as the main character. Some even suggested to the Duffers that they should drop the horror and make it as a mystery caper show for children. It was only really when the producer/director Shawn Levy read the pilot script that things began to fall into place for the Duffers. Levy, who was a big fan of Spielberg and Stephen King, understood exactly what the Duffers wanted to do with the show and helped to broker a deal with Netflix. Who knows what might have happened if Levy hadn't read the Montauk pilot script? Stranger Things might never have made it to the small screen.

(46) We see the characters in season three drinking New Coke. In 1985 Cocoa-Cola changed the formula in their famous soft drink and came up with New Coke - which was intended to be an improvement in terms of taste. Fans of Cocoa-Cola were not impressed though and staged protests. They liked the old Coke just fine and wanted it brought back. After only 79 days, New Coke was given the axe and the original Coke was brought back. The funny thing is though that in blind taste tests New Coke actually got higher scores than Cocoa-

Cola. The intention with New Coke was to make the drink sweeter and keep up with Pepsi. There is a conspiracy theory that this was all a ruse to introduce cheaper corn syrup into Cocoa-Cola but, generally, it seems unlikely that this was all some sort of scam because the company clearly lost money due to the unsold cans and bottles of New Coke. In conjunction with the release of Stranger Things 3, 500,000 cans of New Coke became available online as part of a special promotion. In order to produce these limited editions, the Cocoa-Cola company had to find the New Coke recipe and then produce the drink at its Atlanta bottling plant. Lucas compares New Coke to John Carpenter's The Thing in Stranger Things 3. Classic Coke, according to Lucas, is The Thing From Another World. Both versions are good - simply different. "The original is a classic, no question about it. But the remake - sweeter, bolder, better."

(47) Is Stranger Things a victim of cultural snobbery? Is it too popular for its own good? Consider this. Esquire, AV Club, Radio Times, Forbes and many more didn't even mention Stranger Things 4 when they compiled their list of the best television shows of 2022. The Bear, Andor, Severance, House of Dragon, The White Lotus, The Boys, Our Flag Means Death, and many more shows got mentioned but not Stranger Things 4. On what topsy turvy (cough) upside down planet was Stranger Things 4 not one of the most amazing television shows of 2022?

(48) The music in Stranger Things is usually felt to have been inspired by the classic electronic scores of John Carpenter. One person who would dispute this though is Carpenter himself. The great man, who seemed to be in one of his grumpier moods at the time, said (when he was asked) that the Stranger Things was nothing at all like his own music. Carpenter didn't even seem to know what Stranger Things was - aside from listening to a snatch of the music. Despite the famous composer/director seeking to distance himself from Stranger Things he clearly WAS an influence - though not the only one. Tangerine Dream were equally important - as were Trent Reznor and Nine Inch Nails. The actual theme in the Stranger Things titles is plainly inspired by Wanna Fight from the Only God Forgives soundtrack by Cliff Martinez.

(49) Stranger Things 4 was by far the most expensive season of the

show to produce out of the first four. Netflix don't comment on budgets but according to the Wall Street Journal the fourth season of Stranger Things came in at $30 million an episode - which would put the budget at $270 million. Most big budget Hollywood movies cost less than that to make.

(50) The Duffer Brothers say that one of the reasons why they relate to Stranger Things and created it in the first place is that they were born in 1984 and so were the last generation of kids who grew up (just about) remembering what life was like before the internet and everyone (and I mean EVERYONE) walking around glued to their mobile telephones. The Duffer Brothers had memories of the pre-digital age and liked the idea of a show set in those times. The 1980s seems like a simpler and more pleasant time from our cynical technology obsessed information overload age. Not that the 1980s was perfect. There was more pollution back then and people could smoke anywhere - even in cinemas - so Stranger Things is a somewhat romantic rose-tinted (or neon-tinted if you prefer) depiction of that era but in terms of movies and music it was a great decade. Living in a time when technology was far less dominant in our lives and there was no such thing as angry social media does sound rather lovely from a modern vantage point.

(51) The Satanic Panic mentioned at the end of Stranger Things 3 (which is then part of the plot in season four) was a 1980s phenomenon in which it was alleged that Satanic ritual abuse was rife in the United States and that young minds were being warped by slasher movies, heavy metal music, and Dungeons & Dragons. The evidence for all this moral outrage? Well, there wasn't any. Not a single allegation of Satanic abuse was substantiated. It's hard to say why Dungeons & Dragons was dragged into this hysteria - although a man named Thomas Radecki had a lot to do with it. Radecki was a psychiatrist who was involved in something called the International Coalition Against Violent Entertainment. Radecki seemed to develop a strange vendetta against Dungeons & Dragons and claimed that the game was making young people unhinged and even driving them to suicide. No evidence was found for any of these claims. It appears that Radecki got his evidence from a novel called Mazes & Monsters (which was later adapted into a 1982 film with Tom Hanks). The novel was about teens apparently playing 'live' versions of Dungeons

& Dragons in dangerous underground tunnels. These tales were urban myths though. People who played Dungeons & Dragons did not take the board game into a cave and then get lost or develop hypothermia. They played the game in their bedrooms, classrooms, or (like Mike Wheeler) their basements!

The urban myth seemed to derive from a young man named James Dallas Egbert III who went into an underground tunnel to commit suicide but didn't go through with it and then stayed with friends. The press reported though that he'd gone into caves and tunnels to play Dungeons & Dragons - which was patently not true. These days Thomas Radecki is in prison for abusing some of his patients. Another critic of Dungeons & Dragons was Patricia Pulling. When her son shot himself, Pulling claimed that this was a result of a curse her son had received playing Dungeons & Dragons. She set up a group called B.A.D.D. (Bothered About Dungeons & Dragons). Although Patricia Pullman set herself up as an occult investigator and expert on Dungeons & Dragons her knowledge on the actual game seemed sketchy at best and her claims that there were 300,000 active dangerous Satanists in the United States were ludicrous. Pullman also seemed to think that the Necronomicon (a fictitious 'Demon bible' from the stories of HP Lovecraft) was a real book used by Satanists.

Another high profile 'Satanic panic' incident came in 1986 involving a young man named Sean Sellers. Sean Sellers was born in Corcoran, California, in 1969. In March, 1986, while still a teenager, Sellers killed his mother and stepfather (Vonda and Lee Bellofatto) in Oklahoma City. The victims were asleep at the time. Sellers crept into their room and shot his step-father. He then shot his mother. Sellers then tried to make the house look like it had been robbed. This ruse obviously didn't work. It later transpired that this wasn't the first time Sellers had murdered someone. In 1985 he shot a convenience store clerk who wouldn't sell him any beer. Sellers was arrested fairly swiftly for the murders of these relatives. At the trial he said he was a Satanist and had become possessed by a demon. His lawyers tried to give the impression that he was addicted to Dungeons & Dragons and that this was a factor in the murders. One would think that the best tactic for Sellers' lawyers would have been to plead insanity rather than waffle on about D&D. Sellers later said

himself that Dungeons & Dragons played no part in his crimes.
Sellers was found guilty of multiple homicides and sentenced to
death in 1986. This was a controversial verdict given the young age
of Sean Sellers. The sentence was a result of a quirk in Oklahoma
law which did not give juries the option of giving a life sentence
without the possibility of parole. They were basically giving the jury
two choices. The death penalty OR Sean Sellers probably being
released on parole one day while still a relatively young man. The
jury evidently felt the latter option was too lenient given the nature
of the crimes. Sean Sellers (as ever with murderers and criminals)
found God in prison and said he was no longer a Satanist. He
appeared on television shows and became something of a true crime
celebrity.

There were many appeals against his death sentence and he tried to
argue that he suffered from a personality disorder and therefore
wasn't of sound mind when he was sentenced. The experts could
never quite decide though if Sellers really did have a personality
disorder or was simply a very good actor. Sellers was finally
executed by lethal injection in 1999. He sang Christian music as his
execution loomed. Sellers remains the only person executed in the
United States for a crime committed under the age of 17 since the
reinstatement of the death penalty in 1976. Regarding the D&D
controversies, Dungeons & Dragons co-creator Gary Gygax said -
"Somebody said they threw their copy of D&D; into the fire, and it
screamed. It's a game! The magic spells in it are as real as the gold.
Try retiring on that stuff." Still, if nothing else, all the hysteria over
the game was good for business and simply increased demand for
the game.

(52) The Netflix streaming service overloaded and crashed for about
half an hour when Volume 2 of Stranger Things 4 was dropped on
the site.

(53) It seems as if, for whatever reason, the media are always
looking to anoint a 'Stranger Things Killer' - that is to say a show
that is sort of like Stranger Things but better. Why they should seek
to do this is not readily obvious. Why do shows have to be
compared? Can't we just enjoy them all on their own terms? A show
that was often mentioned in connection to Stranger Things in this

regard was the moody and interesting German series Dark - which had some vague similarities to Stranger Things but was ultimately a very different beast. Another show that some people seemed determined to compare to Stranger Things was Paper Girls - an Amazon show based on the brilliant mystery/science fiction comic book series written by Brian K Vaughan and illustrated by Cliff Chiang. Paper Girls starts in 1988 and revolves around four smart and sassy twelve year-old newspaper delivery girls (Erin, MacKenzie, KJ and Tiffany) who live in Stony Stream, Cleveland. One Halloween, while out delivering newspapers on their bikes early in the morning, they are victims of inexplicable events and become catapulted through time, both past and present, where they meet strange creatures, mysterious beings, and (in the biggest horror of all for a young girl) even their older future selves. Paper Girls (the TV show that is) was enjoyable enough but it was no Stranger Things. This was illustrated by the fact that Amazon axed the show after one season because it hadn't captured enough attention.

(54) In a 2023 article, Indiewire ranked the 15 best episodes of Stranger Things and put The Vanishing of Will Byers (where it all began) at number one. This was slightly unexpected as the season finales tend to be the highest rated but by no means controversial because The Vanishing of Will Byers is a terrific episode. The Vanishing of Will Byers reels us into this world very quickly and the Spielbergian aura (with more than a liberal slosh of Stephen King) is impossible to resist for anyone who loves eighties movies. The characters are all interesting and display believable chemistry with one another and the blending of horror and laughs feels just about right. Stranger Things is scary but not TOO scary. This is PG-13 horror sci-fi in the best tradition. The basic thrust of the plot to carry us forward is the search for Will. This shall draw the boys and Eleven together when they sneak out into the woods at night to look for Will and encounter her in the rain. She's a sodden rain drenched runaway with nowhere to go but for the first time in her life is about to experience friendship.

There are some memorable images and great scenes in this opener. From the horror intro of the doomed scientist and Will's encounter with the monster to Eleven taking refuge in the diner of Benny (Chris Sullivan) where he feeds her ice cream and tries to find out who she is. For the record, the rest of the top five in the Indiewire rankings was (respectively and in order) The Upside Down, The Mind Flayer, Dear Billy, and The Bathtub. The highest ranked season three episode is The Battle of Starcourt at number nine (which tends to suggest that season three did not produce as many classic episodes as the other seasons).

(55) David Harbour said that during the production of season one, Winona Ryder acted as a sort of 1980s Wikipedia for the Duffers and pointed out anachronisms in the script to them. She was especially savvy when it came to household products and music.

(56) Is there a Commando costume Easter egg in Stranger Things 2 that no one seems to notice? Commando is a 1985 action film starring Arnold Schwarzenegger as a retired special forces soldier named John Matrix who has to rescue his daughter Jenny when she is kidnapped. Commando is the film that established the Arnold movie 'persona' and a ludicrously enjoyable park your brain at the door action film in which Schwarzenegger kills an estimated eighty one people with an assortment of deadly weapons. Anyway, Eleven's overalls and curly hair in Stranger Things 2 are suspiciously similar to Alyssa Milano as Jenny Matrix in Commando. This surely can't be a coincidence can it?

(57) What in the name of Jim Hopper is Planck's constant? The finale of Stranger Things 3 needs an answer fast. From the Encyclopaedia Britannica - 'Planck's constant, (symbol h), fundamental physical constant characteristic of the mathematical formulations of quantum mechanics, which describes the behaviour of particles and waves on the atomic scale, including the particle aspect of light. The German physicist Max Planck introduced the constant in 1900 in his accurate formulation of the distribution of the radiation emitted by a blackbody, or perfect absorber of radiant energy (see Planck's radiation law). The significance of Planck's constant in this context is that radiation, such as light, is emitted, transmitted, and absorbed in discrete energy packets, or quanta, determined by the frequency of the radiation and the value of Planck's constant. The energy E of each quantum, or each photon, equals Planck's constant h times the radiation frequency symbolized by the Greek letter nu, ν, or simply $E = h\nu$. A modified form of

Planck's constant called h-bar ($\hbar$), or the reduced Planck's constant, in which $\hbar$ equals h divided by 2π, is the quantization of angular momentum. For example, the angular momentum of an electron bound to an atomic nucleus is quantized and can only be a multiple of h-bar.' Well, that's certainly cleared that one up hasn't it?

(58) In April 2022, images from the new edition of the Stranger Things Monopoly game appeared on social media and apparently sent the Duffers in a 'meltdown' because they divulged some secrets about the forthcoming fourth season. The Monopoly images revealed that Eleven has her short hair back and goes to a top secret desert lab, that Hopper escapes from prison on a snowmobile, and that Eddie stages an impromptu concert to ward off bats.

(59) The kiss between Hopper and Joyce in season four wasn't scripted or planned. It was improvised by David Harbour and Winona Ryder.

(60) Notice that Eleven has a scar on her shin in the roller rink in season four. This is from where the Flayer parasite was removed in season three.

(61) Stranger Things 4 accrued 7.2 billion minutes of streaming viewership in the United States from May 30 to June 5 in 2022.

(62) Noah Schnapp was up for the part of Richie Tozier in Stephen King's IT before Finn Wolfhard was cast. In a quirk of casting coincidence, Schnapp and Wolfhard were both cast in Stranger Things soon after. Noah also auditioned to play Mike Wheeler in Stranger Things too so you might say he lost TWO jobs to Finn Wolfhard. It all worked out for Noah in the end though because he got the part of Will Byers.

(63) Gwinnett Place Mall on the outskirts of Atlanta was used for the Starcourt Mall in season three. This mall opened in 1984 but it had fallen on hard times in recent years through a combination of larger more modern malls opening in the area and the popularity of online shopping. It was more or less abandoned when the Stranger Things production team found it. Netflix leased about 30% of the mall and created 40 realistic stores - in addition to cleaning the place up and

making it look like a real 1985 shopping mall. They even put in an operational food court. This all took about six weeks - which was a remarkable effort. There was hope that Netflix might leave their renovations and props in place and allow the mall to become a Stranger Things tourist attraction. This didn't happen though and all the props were taken away. To be fair to Netflix they were probably worried about thieves stealing valuable props and the prohibitive cost of security was something they were understandably eager to remove from their expenses. Gwinnett Place Mall therefore became rather neglected again. In 2022 it was announced that a $1 billion project to revamp the mall and its land (around 40% of Gwinnett Place Mall was made up of parking space) into a scheme called 'Global Villages' would go ahead. The plan is to build a park, retail stores, a cultural centre, 3,000 homes, and more besides on the site. Time will tell if this ambitious project comes to fruition.

(64) Why is the science teacher Mr Clarke not in Stranger Things 4? There seems to be no valid reason. Granted, the kids are not in Middle School anymore but surely they could have found a way for him to make a cameo. Couldn't Mr Clarke have turned up at the end as one of the emergency volunteers? Did you know by the way that in the original plan for Stranger Things the character of Mr Clarke was going to be very different indeed? Mr Clarke was going to be a handsome young teacher who plays a pivotal role in battling the Upside Down. In short, Mr Clarke was going to be a major character at the heart of the show. The original conception for Scott Clarke then was clearly to make him the Hawkins version of Indiana Jones. While this idea tickled the Spielberg obsessed Duffers they obviously decided in the end not to go through with this idea.

Mr Clarke was very different when the show hit the screen and a nerdy beloved science teacher - as opposed to an action hero. It would appear most likely that the Duffers decided that if Hawkins had a version of Indiana Jones fighting the Upside Down and solving mysteries then this might detract from other characters - especially Hopper for example. Hopper would no longer be the male lead in the show if Scott Clarke was Indiana Jones. Randy Havens had a fairly substantial role in season one as Mr Clarke but this didn't last. His role in season three consisted of one cameo scene and, as we just noted, he didn't appear in season four at all. Many fans think that Mr

Clarke is something of a wasted character in the show. With his knowledge of science might it not have been enjoyable to see Mr Clarke become aware and involved in the Upside Down battles? If you are a fan of Mr Clarke and think he's been sidelined in the show you might enjoy the comic Stranger Things: The Tomb of Ybwen. In the story some of the boys discover that Bob Newby left a treasure map behind so set off in search of the coordinates. When they get caught in a blizzard it is up to Mr Clarke to save them.

(65) There is a nice and very deliberate irony to Jason Carver's deranged warnings about cults in Stranger Things 4 because Jason clearly has all the makings of a cult leader himself. He's charismatic, somewhat unhinged, persuasive, a leader, convinced that he is always right about everything, and absolutely loves making speeches. This kid is truly in love with the sound of his own voice. You could even say that Jason is already a cult leader with his brainwashed basketball players willing to swallow literally anything he tells them. Jason is clearly someone who has been taking all these Satanic panic headlines to heart in a most unhealthy and misguided way.

(66) The Freddy Funko range of Steve Harrington figures can go for surprisingly high prices. Some collectors put these for sale at $500.

(67) Vecna was a wizard in Dungeons & Dragons. The character is known as the God of Secrets. Vecna was first referenced in OD&D's third supplement, Eldritch Wizardry. The character is a lich and ruler of the Occluded Empire of Vecna. A 'lich' is an Old English word for an undead person. The word was used in the Lovecraft story The Thing on the Doorstep and obviously features in Dungeons & Dragons. Vecna follows in the tradition of Stranger Things villains in that it is inspired by Dungeons & Dragons but not strictly the same thing as its board game counterpart. A big influence on Vecna in Stranger Things was the Night King in Game of Thrones.

(68) Millie Bobby Brown said that when her parents heard about the casting for a show called Montauk (obviously later to be called Stranger Things) she wasn't very keen to do an audition and was tired of acting and rejections but her parents told her if she did this one last audition she could then go out and play and do whatever she

wanted. Millie therefore relented and agreed to do a cam audition. Millie deciding to do that audition was what you call a true 'sliding doors' moment because it led to her becoming a world famous millionaire and highly successful and much in demand young actor. Who knows what might have happened if she hadn't done the Montauk audition? She might have drifted out of acting altogether and done something completely different with her life.

(69) There are some mistakes in the Hawkins Family Video store in season three in that some of the videos are not in the boxes they would have been in 1985. The copies of Truck Turner and Five Deadly Venoms are from the 1990s and the copy of Mad Max we see is from a later re-release.

(70) The Last of Us, a 2013 video game about a journey across a post-apocalyptic United States, features a girl named Ellie. This is a possible source of inspiration for Eleven's name in Stranger Things. The Duffers, who are big video game fans, have openly cited The Last of Us as an inspiration for their approach to Stranger Things. There is a connection between Stranger Things and The Last of Us in that Millie Bobby Brown and Bella Ramsey both went up for the same role in Game of Thrones (with Ramsey obviously winning the part). Years later Bella Ramsey would be cast as Ellie in the HBO television adaptation of The Last of Us.

(71) Vecna's body is nowhere to be found after he is blasted out of the window by Nancy's shotgun in the season four finale. This is a homage to the body of Michael Myers vanishing after he is shot by Loomis at the end of John Carpenter's Halloween. Vecna and Michael Myers are, to say the least, both rather difficult to put down for the count.

(72) David Harbour as Hopper has 233 fewer lines in season four than he did in season three. His role in Stranger Things 4 is greatly reduced compared to previous seasons.

(73) According to the Hollywood Reporter, the child actors in Stranger Things were paid $20,000 an episode in season one. That's peanuts compared to what they get now.

(74) In season four the show switched from RED, the established camera for Stranger Things, to the ARRI Alexa. The intention is to give each season a slightly different palette so it made sense to change cameras. Season one is autumnal, season two is blue, misty and moody, season three is neon, and season four is dreamlike and eclectic.

(75) Shooting on Stranger Things 4 was halted after a couple of weeks in March 2020 due to the pandemic and only resumed again in September. Millie Bobby Brown had only just had her costume fitting session when the season was put on ice so the cancellation for her was especially frustrating.

(76) Jamie Campbell Bower had to spend eight hours in make-up to transform himself into Vecna. The production staff said he bore this ordeal with great patience and good humour.

(77) A mint condition Barb Holland Lego can go for $400 on the net.

(78) Joseph Quinn had no idea that Eddie was going to die when he signed up for Stranger Things 4. This has parallels with Shannon Purser - who didn't know that Barb was going to shuffle off this mortal coil by way of a Demogorgon in the Harrington pool when she signed up for season one. Shannon got her first inkling that Barb was Upside Down toast when she heard someone discussing her death scene while she was in make-up.

(79) Eleven has her season one buzzcut back in season four but this time they didn't shave Millie Bobby Brown's hair off. What they did instead was slick Millie's hair back and stuff it under a short haired wig.

(80) Oddly, despite playing Carter Burke in Aliens and Dr Sam Owens in Stranger Things, Paul Reiser said he doesn't actually like science fiction and never watches this sort of stuff in real life. It's just not his cup of tea.

(81) The singer Limahl had never actually heard of Stranger Things before his song The Neverending Story was used in Stranger Things 3. Limahl said he only realised the show was a big deal when he

asked his much younger relatives about it.

(82) It was reported in 2023 that David Harbour and Winona Ryder would both receive $9.5 million for Stranger Things 5. This was over four times what they had received for season one way back in 2015. Millie Bobby Brown's salary for season five was more mysterious as it came as part of a Netflix contract that she'd signed a few years before. You could be certain that Millie wouldn't be getting chump change for season five though. By now she was said to have a personal net worth of $15 million - which is not bad going for a nineteen year-old. One entertainment site even ventured that Millie would be getting $20 million for Stranger Things 5 - which would be remarkable if true.

(83) The Creel House in Stranger Things 4 is really the Claremont House in Rome, Georgia. This seven bedroom house was built in 1882. Late in 2022, it was reported that the house was up for sale at an asking price of $1.5 million. So, if you have $1.5 million burning a hole in your pocket then a slice of Stranger Things history could be yours. The Claremont House appealed to the Duffers because it rather evoked The Well House, also known as the Haunted House, in Stephen King's IT.

(84) One of the Stranger Things 4 production units began production under the secret codename Tareco. Tareco is a type of biscuit popular in parts of Brazil. The codename was obviously done to try and dodge any spoilers. It is fairly common for highly anticipated films and TV shows to shoot under a secret codename as a means to (hopefully) throw the media off their trail.

(85) Stranger Things 4 required an incredible 300 days of shooting before it was in the can. The cast must have felt like they had been shooting it forever when they were finally allowed to depart and move onto other things. The length of the shoot was a testament to how ambitious season was with the larger than usual cast and electric range of shooting locations - Atlanta, New Mexico, Lithuania.

(86) Stranger Things 4 was the first season of the show to be released in two parts. Previous seasons were dropped on Netflix in

their entirety and rabidly binged in short order from start to finish by fans. It was widely assumed at the time that some cynical Netflix number crunching was responsible for the season being split into two parts. The theory was that Netflix wanted to stop people unsubscribing after watching Stranger Things 4 - so they split it up. You'd now have to keep Netflix in order to watch the rest of the season (or two episodes to be precise) at a later date. It turned out though that this presumption wasn't actually correct. The reason why we had to wait for the last batch of episodes is that the special effects were still being tweaked. The last episode of season four, according to the Duffers, had more digital effects shots than the previous three seasons all put together.

(87) The only two characters with over 300 lines in season four are Dustin Henderson and Steve Harrington.

(88) Robert Englund, the horror icon who plays Victor Creel in Stranger Things 4, was not someone that the production team reached out to. In fact, it was the other way around. Englund sent in an audition tape for season four and the Duffers, who are clearly HUGE fans of A Nightmare On Elm Street, were amazed to suddenly see Englund as they waded through the tapes of actors aspiring to be in season four. Legend has it that Englund taped his audition in the bath.

(89) Hopper's firearm in season two is a Colt Python. This is the gun that Rick Grimes uses in The Walking Dead. It is also the gun that George C. Scott uses in the film version of Firestarter. The book and film of Stephen King's Firestarter was clearly a big influence on Stranger Things. The plot revolves around a young girl who has pyrokinetic abilities because her parents were subject to an MKUltra type experiment when they were teenagers. There are many ideas in Firestarter that Stranger Things uses - like the girl (named Charlie) having nosebleeds and wearing electronic equipment on her head to monitor her during experiments. A Colt Python is also but one of many weapons used by Gordon Freeman in Half-Life. Half-Life is a classic 1998 first-person shooter video game developed by Valve and published by Sierra Studios for Microsoft Windows in 1998. Half-Life revolves around a physicist named Gordon Freeman who works at the top secret Black Mesa Research Facility. An accident at

the facility creates a resonance cascade that opens up a portal to another dimension. Creatures from this other dimension invade the facility through the dimensional rifts. The only way to solve this crisis is to close the rift to the alien dimension - and this will involve a trip to the nightmarish Xen. Half-Life has more or less the same plot as the early seasons of Stranger Things and it's impossible to play the game now and not think of the show. This is especially the case when Gordon Freeman encounters the portal and strange alien creatures are appearing through the haze. Just to add to the connections, Half-Life was inspired by Stephen King's The Mist and an Outer Limits episode called The Borderland - both of which were an influence on Stranger Things. Teen villain Jason Carver also uses a Colt Python in Stranger Things 4 - though he is plainly too young to legally purchase one.

(90) The attitude of the Stranger Things cast to the show ending after season five seems to be a general air of sadness but also agreement and acceptance. David Harbour, Finn Wolfhard, and Sadie Sink have all said that it is time for the cast and the Duffers to move onto new things and the next chapter in their careers. They will miss the show but they think it is better to get out while the going is good rather than run the risk of going on for too long and running out of story and maybe viewers too.

(91) The big winners in the cast in terms of a career boost through the immense popularity of the show have been David Harbour and Millie Bobby Brown. Harbour has been in several movies since Stranger Things lifted him out of his supporting player purgatory while Millie has appeared in two Godzilla movies and also the popular Enola Holmes adaptations for Netflix. Brown is also going to be in The Electric State for the Russo Brothers and play the lead in the fantasy action caper Damsel. Millie Bobby Brown has become a bona fide star and she still isn't out of her teens. Sadie Sink is also carving out a strong career and has appeared in productions like Fear Street and The Whale. Finn Wolfhard has also made a number of movies (most notably Ghostbusters: Afterlife) although his role in the big screen version of Stephen King's IT was actually secured before he became famous through Stranger Things. Finn has already directed a short film and it is suspected that he might actually end up behind the camera rather than in front of it. The Duffers say that

Finn has used Stranger Things as a sort of film school crash course and soaked up as much information about the nuts and bolts of shooting and production as possible. Gaten Matarazzo has done less screen acting than his co-stars off the back of Stranger Things but this mainly because he has hosted the Netflix show Prank Encounters and also gone back to his first love - the stage.

(92) The sequence where Chrissy, thanks to the unwelcome attention of Vecna, hallucinates in nightmarish fashion in the first episode of season four is an explicit nod to the film Nightmare On Elm Street 3: Dream Warriors.

(93) David Harbour said that when they about halfway through shooting season one the person doing his hair in makeup commented that the show wasn't working and would probably be a disaster. David said there was a general sense on season one that this show wouldn't get much attention and would not get a second season.

(94) When she became famous, Millie Bobby Brown was rather bemused and baffled by the amount of American interviewers who thought she was Australian. Australian and English accents must presumably sound the same to some Americans?

(95) For the scenes in Stranger Things 4 where Eleven is in the sensory deprivation chamber water tank they had to use an overhead Technocrane because it was impossible to put a camera in that sealed environment.

(96) When we learn the origin of Vecna/Henry Creel in The Massacre at Hawkins Lab, the music playing is by by Philip Glass from the film Koyaanisqatsi. Koyaanisqatsi is a cult 1982 film directed by Godfrey Reggio with music by award winning composer Philip Glass and cinematography by Ron Fricke. The film is a visual documentary featuring time lapse photography. Although this is a film with no dialogue and no plot, Koyaanisqatsi still has a story to tell. It's more a piece of art than a film and if the purpose of art is to take us out of the everyday world and make us look at something in a slightly different way than Koyaanisqatsi fulfils this specific criteria. A message of the film is obviously an environmental one but it also seems to marvel at times at man's technological ingenuity and

progress and perhaps the real subtext is that with all our advances and technology it's sad that we haven't created a better or more peaceful world to live in where people are more equal - the film including a segment that includes a pointed and varied tapestry of human life contrasting street beggars to privileged posh folk ready for a night on the town.

The film suggests that our artificial environments have created a form of madness with people resembling nothing more than cattle at times. The slow motion is extraordinary at times with the stirring music by Glass and there is some striking stock footage of the destruction of large buildings and images of housing projects in deep decay. Footage of military devastation also features in Koyaanisqatsi with endless lines of Soviet tanks, bombs, aircraft carriers (with sailors in formation spelling out the equation $E = mc2$) and cities in rubble. The film becomes more hypnotic and trippy when it speeds up the footage with cars driving around cities at night, illuminated by their vaporous light trails in the darkness. Traffic and pollution are highlighted with people chasing around in circles on motorways, traffic patterns seen from high above and an overview of a huge car park. Man is trapped in a gigantic circuitous mechanised rat race and therefore unable to fully appreciate the world around him. We see people shuffling to work and doing repetitive tasks on factory production duties, standing on escalators in New York's Grand Central Terminal and manufacturing cars on monstrous assembly lines. Intercut with this are people shopping during leisure time to illustrate the circular nature of life and continue the film's rumination on technology and how it may have made us even more constricted instead of liberating us.

The city sequences contain a wonderful image of the moon passing behind a skyscraper and satellite photography. The Glass music used in the Creel documentary was also used in Zack Snyder's Watchman adaption for the scenes where Jon Osterman is transformed into the God like being Dr Manhattan

(97) There are essentially three different movies at the heart of Stranger Things 4. There is Hopper in Russia, Eleven and the Byers family in California, and then the other regulars in good old Hawkins. In this case though it would (as ever) be scary old

Hawkins. The three broad stories in season four are then, in the traditional fashion, tied together. Each of these plot strands had their own unique influences. Hopper's arc draws on prison movies but also sci-fi horror like Alien 3 (which is a prison movie too), Splice, and The Thing. The Byers family in California draws on - among others - Spielberg, The Lost Boys, and teen outcast dramas. The Hawkins scenes draw on everything from Hellraiser to A Nightmare On Elm Street to haunted house movies to serial killer movies to Red Dawn.

(98) The season two episode The Lost Sister is the only episode in the show's history to have an overwhelmingly negative reputation. This is the episode where Eleven travels to Chicago to track down Kali and then becomes part of a gang seeking to extract revenge against those who worked at the Hawkins Department of Energy. The problem with the episode is not so much that it is amazingly bad per se but more the fact that it feels out of place. We are suddenly yanked out of Hawkins and have to watch an entire episode where - apart from Eleven - we don't know any of these characters from Adam. Stranger Things 2 had built up an impressive head of steam by this point with the intrigue at the Hawkins Lab and it feels like a chore to have to sit through The Lost Sister before we can go back to Hawkins again. Though the Duffers defended the episode at the time it is notable that Kali hasn't been used since - not even in the Brenner/lab centric season four. That probably tells you all you need to know about how successful The Lost Sister was. Stranger Things is usually excellent at quickly establishing new characters (Eddie, Bob Newby, Max, Robin, Dr Owens etc) but Kali seemed to represent a rare fumble for the Duffers. The character of Kali, for whatever reason, just wasn't that interesting or memorable.

(99) The design of Vecna patently owes something to The Gill-Man in Creature from the Black Lagoon. Creature from the Black Lagoon (what a great name for a film) was released in 1954 and directed by Jack Arnold from a screenplay by Harry Essex. In the lush and somewhat foreboding environment of the Amazonian rain forest Dr Carl Maia (Antonio Moreno) makes a most extraordinary discovery. A fossilized hand with fins and claws no less. He decides to put a team together to travel down river to the mythic Black Lagoon in search of more evidence of this uncanny nature. Saddling up are Dr

David Reed (Richard Carlson), Reed's girlfriend Kay Lawrence
(Julie Adams), Dr Mark Williams (Richard Denning), and Dr Edwin
Thompson (Whit Bissel). But Lucas (Nestor Paiva) - the Captain of
their chartered boat "Rita" - tells them about the spooky legend of
the man-fish that that resides at the Black Lagoon. A humanoid
creature with gills and scales. Like a cross between a lizard, a fish
and a synchronized swimmer.

They all soon realise that this apparently ludicrous tale is all too true
and eventually make unpleasant contact with "The Gill-Man"
(played by Ben Chapman on land and Ricou Browning underwater),
resulting in more than a few deaths. The jungle bound boffins are
soon arguing over whether or not capture the creature, kill it, or just
leave it alone and get out of the lagoon and the jungle altogether.
Spielberg's classic Jaws actually paid homage to Creature From the
Black Lagoon by aping the device of taking us closer and closer to a
potential victim from under the water. The creature is not exactly
state of the art all these decades on but it has real personality and a
compelling quality. This film plays like a fusion of The Lost World
and an underwater King Kong and although he isn't always much of
a gentleman you do feel some sympathy for the Gill-Man as the
humans are invading his habitat and he's only defending his home
really.

(100) The original name for the Mind Flayer was the Shadow
Monster. The Duffer Brothers got the idea of calling the entity the
Mind Flayer from a monster in Dungeons & Dragons. The Flayer in
Stranger Things 2 doesn't resemble its D&D namesake much
visually but it does share similar telepathic abilities. 'Mind flayers
are found only in subterranean places, as they detest sunlight,' wrote
Gary Gygax, the co-creator of D&D.'"They are greatly evil and
consider the bulk of humanity (and its kin) as cattle to feed upon.
These monsters speak only their own arcane language and several
other weird tongues — purportedly those of terrible races of things
which dwell in regions of the subterranean world far deeper than
mankind has ever ventured. It is also rumored that these monsters
have a city somewhere deep beneath the earth. ... Its skin color is a
nauseous mauve, its tentacles being purplish black. A mind flayer's
eyes are dead white, no pupil being evident. The three long fingers
of each hand are reddish, but the hands are mauve.'

(101) David Harbour said that when he was shooting season one he didn't interact with anyone much and sat in his house alone after shooting. It was his way of getting into the headspace of Hopper - who is still very raw and damaged in season one because of the loss of his daughter.

(102) Max mentions Ted Bundy in season four when she debates Eddie's guilt with Dustin. As you know, Ted Bundy is probably the most famous serial killer in American true crime history. Hawkins experiences something of a serial killer 'panic' in the wake of Chrissy's death (apparently at the hands of Eddie - though we know poor Eddie is innocent) and this is surprisingly realistic as a plot development because in the mid 1980s the United States had more serial killers than at any time before or since. Serial killers today are at a low level compared to the 1970s and 1980s.

There are a number of factors for why this is the case. The fact that most nations have extensive CCTV camera systems in cities and towns now is one obvious reason why it's harder to be a serial killer today. If someone like Richard Ramirez or Ted Bundy was prowling suspiciously round some neighbourhood today they'd be picked up on multiple cameras very quickly. It would be very difficult today, for example, to break into an apartment building without being captured on camera. Home security systems and alarms are also better than they used to be. Most homes also have outdoor security lighting today. Another reason for why there aren't as many serial killers now is that the police have more technology at their disposal and are simply better at catching murderers than they used to be. Forensics and DNA profiling is much more advanced today than it was in the 1980s. If some of the more infamous serial killers from yesteryear were operating today they would almost certainly be captured a lot more quickly. The police today can convict someone from a single strand of hair found at a crime scene. This sort of forensic technology means that serial killers today have no margin of error at all anymore.

Another reason as to why serial killer murders are not as common as they used to be is that modern society is less risk adverse than it was in the 1970s and 1980s. People and (especially) teenagers and children are more clued up about danger. Society, for better or worse, is less innocent than it used to be. Children and young people also go out less than they used. In the 1960s and 1970s it was common for teenagers and children to go out and roam free for hours. Nowadays, this doesn't happen so much. Children and young people tend to stay home more (where they have social media and ample entertainment technology). In the 1980s it was also fairly common for young women to hitchhike alone and take a lift from men they didn't know - which sounds crazy today. People of all ages now also have mobile phones too so are always in contact and easy to trace. Even cars have a GPS now. All these things make it a lot more difficult to be a serial killer than it used to be. In 1986 though these things didn't apply. The people of Hawkins were therefore more susceptible to a serial killer panic - like the one whipped up by Jason Carver.

(103) When she got the part of Max Mayfield in season two, Sadie Sink had to learn how to use a skateboard. This was no easy task because she'd never used a skateboard in her life and her first attempt didn't go well when she took a heavy fall. She had some secret help though from another cast member. Finn Wolfhard turned out to be something of a skateboard ace and joined Sadie Sink on her skateboard lessons to lend assistance and offer some handy tips.

(104) Stranger Things fans love fan theories in the preamble to a new season. The show lends itself to this sort of thing because conspiracies are woven into its DNA. A lot of these fan theories are wide of the mark but they can be surprisingly accurate too. Online detectives can decode a surprising amount - even from episode titles. There have been a number of fan theories though which turned out to be idle speculation and little more. So what are the most fun but misguided fan theories related to Stranger Things? One fan theory circa Stranger Things 2 was the suggestion that Billy and Max are the unwitting children of Soviet spies living in the United States (as in The Americans - which Sadie Sink was actually in). The genesis of this theory was the fact that Billy and Max and their family were rather on the vague side in season two and we didn't learn much about them.

This detail was conflated with the fact that Murry Bauman seemed to believe there was a Soviet conspiracy in Hawkins. Another enjoyable fan theory in relation to Max was the belief that she was one of the super powered children from Brenner's lab. The evidence for this theory was that Max seemed to wear long sleeves in season two - thus conveniently covering a tattoo with her number. Another piece of evidence tied - less convincingly - into this theory was the fact that in one of the Stranger Things computer games Max could emit telekinetic blasts. Did the makers of that game know something we didn't? Well, no, not really. Another early fan theory, though not a popular one, was the assertion that Murray Bauman was a Soviet spy. Murray is many things - chef, martial artist, impressionist - but he's definitely not a Soviet spy.

(105) 250 wigs were used during the production of Stranger Things 4.

(106) Matthew Modine turned down the part of Dr Brenner several times before he finally relented and agreed to do it. To be fair to Modine he probably had no idea who the Duffers were at the time and how was he to know that the show was going to be so popular and good?

(107) Levon Thurman-Hawke - younger brother of Maya Hawke - has a cameo in Stranger Things 4 as a customer in the background at the Family Video store where Steve and Robin work. Levon is made to look quite punkish so look out for a punk who resembles Maya Hawke and this cameo should be easy to spot. This was not the first Family Video cameo in the show. In the finale of season three the show's music composers Michael Stein and Kyle Dixon can be seen as browsing customers at the Family Video store when Steve and Robin ask Keith if he has any jobs available.

(108) One of the people who does the subtitles for Stranger Things said that using the words 'tentacles undulating moistly' to describe the sound effects of Vecna in his lair was done as a bit of a joke.

(109) Although the Tolkien estate took legal action against Dungeons & Dragons for its obvious similarities to The Hobbit and The Lord of the Rings, Gary Gygax, the co-creator of D&D, claimed that he disliked Tolkien's books and found them dull.

(110) Some fans think that Stranger Things 2 missed a trick by not
having Polybius in the Palace Arcade. Polybius is a fictitious arcade
game and the subject of an urban myth. The urban legend describes
the game as part of a government-run psychology experiment based
in Portland, Oregon, during 1981. Gameplay supposedly produced
intense psychoactive and addictive effects in the player. These few
publicly staged arcade machines were said to have been visited
periodically by men in black for the purpose of data-mining the
machines and analyzing these effects. Eventually, all of these
Polybius arcade machines allegedly disappeared from the arcade
market.

(111) Stranger Things 4 used a number of production codenames for
secrecy. When it started shooting in Atlanta it was disguised as a
production named Weyland. This was a reference to Weyland-
Yutani - which is the name of the sinister corporation in the Alien
movie franchise. The name Weyland-Yutani was created by Ron
Cobb for Alien. Cobb imagined a big British company like British
Leyland merging with a big Japanese company - and so came up
with Weyland-Yutani. This production codename was very apt
because Stranger Things is deluged with references to the Alien
franchise. The Spy, which is episode six of Stranger Things 2, is
Stranger Things in complete Aliens tribute mode with the
Demogorgons attacking the soldiers in the tunnels, motion trackers,
and video camera point of view footage. Aliens was named as the
biggest influence on Stranger Things 2 by the Duffer Brothers in that
they wanted to do a sequel that was still part of the Stranger Things
universe but also bigger and slightly different - just like Aliens.

We must mention too that Eleven's curly hair at the start of Stranger
Things 2 seems to be inspired by Sigourney Weaver's hairstyle in
Aliens. Stranger Things also has three cast members who were in
Alien films - Paul Reiser, Winona Ryder, and Amy Seimetz. Seimetz
played Eleven's aunt Becky in the show and was in Alien: Covenant.

(112) Gaten Materazzo's shaggy hair in Stranger Things is a
stipulation from the producers. He is asked to grow his hair out when
a new season is due to commence production. As soon as shooting is
over he usually gets his hair cut because he doesn't especially enjoy
having long hair in real life. A lot of the cast in the show have used

wigs to depict the 1980s hair of their characters. Dacre Montgomery and Charlie Heaton both used hair pieces in the show as Billy and Jonathan respectively because their own hair was too short. Ditto for David Harbour - though only in season two. Noah Schaap's Dumb and Dumber bowl cut as Will Byers is also a hairpiece.

(113) Seasons one, two and three all have three episodes in the top ten highest rated Stranger Things episodes on IMDB. Stranger Things 3, by contrast, only has one episode in the top ten - the season finale The Battle of Starcourt. This would suggest that IMDB voters tended to feel that season three wasn't as consistently strong as the other seasons.

(114) It seems plausible to speculate that the Stranger Things 4 music supervisor Nora Felder might have got the idea to use a Kate Bush song from the 1988 John Hughes film She's Having a Baby. She's Having a Baby uses the Kate Bush song 'This Woman's Work' for an especially emotional montage sequence

(115) The house in Fayetteville, Georgia used for the Byers home is actually over a hundred years old. It was perfect for the rural ramshackle look they wanted. Only the exteriors were used though. The interior scenes were shot in the studio back in Atlanta.

(116) At the end of Stranger Things 2, Dustin put a DemoDog in the fridge. This was expected by some fans to perhaps be laying the ground for some sort of subplot in season three but the DemoDog was never mentioned again. It seems that the Duffers never intended this to amount to anything or simply forgot about it (which isn't impossible because in Stranger Things 4 they famously forgot when Will's birthday is supposed to be). One of the comics provided as good an explanation as any for what happened to the DemoDog by revealing that it turned to liquid sludge in the fridge and was therefore lost to medical science (as Dustin had presumably intended).

(117) For continuity purposes, David Harbour shot his season four flashbacks of Hopper surviving the drilling machine explosion at the end of season three. This needed to be done because he had to lose a lot of weight to portray Hopper in a Soviet prison.

(118) Dimitri, the prison guard who eventually teams up with Hopper in Stranger Things 4, was originally going to be killed off but this was changed and he survived the season in the end.

(119) The futuristic bathing costume that Eleven wears in the lab scenes in season one of Stranger Things and in Stranger Things 4 is a haptic suit. Haptic technology is technology that can create an experience of touch by applying forces, vibrations, or motions to the user. The suit in season one was biege and had rectangle blocks which acted as weights so that Eleven could sink into the sensory deprivation water tank. In season four the suit was white to make it more stark in the underground lab and the rectangle blocks on the suit were actually floats so that Eleven could float in the water tank. The concept behind the suit is that this is essentially Eleven's superhero costume.

(120) Stranger Things 4 was the most watched Netflix show in 92 countries. Such is the global appeal of the show that some industry commentators wonder how on earth Netflix will cope when this pop culture juggernaut comes to an end. How can they possibly replace Stranger Things?

(121) When they designed the look of the Upside Down in Stranger Things the production design team spent a lot of time researching mildew and the microscopic photography of organisms.

(122) In the original concept for Joyce Byers was a loud Long Island waitress who didn't suffer fools gladly. The relocation of the show from Long Island to Indiana and the casting of Winona Ryder changed all of these plans. Winona asked if the character could be like Richard Dreyfuss in Close Encounters of the Third Kind - which is to say an ordinary person engulfed in a mystery and obsession beyond their comprehension which they must solve in an instinctive rather than rational way. Steve Harrington was a lot nastier in the early plans for the show but the Duffers decided to spin the character on his head and make him a hero rather than a villain in the end. The reason they did this is because they were enjoying the charisma and comic timing Joe Keery was bring to the part and wanted to find a way to make him a main character. Apart from the abandoned concept of having Mr Clarke be like Indiana Jones, the biggest

change was that in the early plans for the show the character of Terry
Ives was not Eleven's mother but a conspiracy theorist described as
being bald with huge glasses. This character eventually became
Murray Bauman - who was introduced in season two.

(123) The Duffers give the character of Robin a lot of expositional
dialogue in the show because Maya Hawke can talk really fast and
so will rattle though this stuff quicker than anyone else.

(124) Noah Schnapp launched his own vegan chocolate hazelnut
spread in 2022. The product is called tbh - which stands for 'to be
honest'. The ingredients in Noah's healthier more eco friendly
version of that famous 'other' chocolate spread are - hazelnuts,
organic sugar, pea protein, sunflower oil, soluble corn fiber, organic
cocoa powder, cocoa butter, cocoa liquor, sunflower lecithin, natural
flavors, and monk fruit.

(125) We don't actually see Will Byers do his school presentation at
the start of Stranger Things 4 but we see evidence that it was going
to be about Alan Turing. Alan Turing was a British mathematician,
computer scientist, logician, cryptanalyst, philosopher, and
theoretical biologist. He played a vital role for the Allies in cracking
the German codes during World War 2. Sadly, Turing lived during a
time when it was much more difficult to be gay. This contributed to
his suicide at the age of 42.

(126) Caleb McLaughlin said he doesn't like rehearsing scenes
because he prefers to get into the 'moment' and be more spontaneous.
One scene he was happy to rehearse though was the fight between
Lucas and Jason Carver in season four. Caleb and Mason Dye did
extensive rehearsals for this fight to make it as realistic as possible.

(127) The device used in the lab by Brenner in Stranger Things 4 to
inhibit Henry's powers is called a soteria. In Greek mythology,
Soteria was the goddess or spirit (daimon) of safety and salvation,
deliverance, and preservation from harm.

(128) The house in California where Joyce Byers lives in Stranger
Things 4 was found by the production crew in Albuquerque's
Glenwood Hills community. They had originally planned to

construct a house themselves but found exactly what they were looking for as this real house had Poltergeist/E.T Spielberg vibes and also outdated fittings and fixtures which made it already feel like a period home even before anything was done. About a month after season wrapped, the house was put on the market and became an Airbnb starting at $400 a night.

(129) Sadie Sink was allowed to take home and keep the Walkman that Max uses in season four to listen top Kate Bush.

(130) There seems to be a Jeffrey Dahmer Easter egg in season four when Max gets off the bus and a kid who looks the dead spit of Dahmer (right down to the aviator spectacles) walks past in the background. Dahmer was a notorious serial killer and cannibal. The miniseries Monster: The Jeffrey Dahmer Story dropped on Netflix in fairly close proximity to Stranger Things 4 so this doesn't seem like a coincidence. The Duffers have not officially acknowledged if the kid REALLY was supposed to a Dahmer reference though.

(131) The cemetery which features in the episode Dear Billy is really Stone Mountain Cemetery in Stone Mountain, Georgia. This location was previously used for Barb's funeral in season two.

(132) Joe Keery originally tested for the part of Jonathan Byers in the show. About three months later he was contacted again and asked to audition for Steve Harrington. Joe said that Steve was described to him as 'Nancy's jerk boyfriend'.

(133) Gaten Matarazzo said it was a great relief to him that the Kate Bush song Running Up That Hill became a big deal in season four because people finally stopped going on about the Neverending Story song he had to sing in season three!

(134) Brett Gelman said he trained in karate for three months to prepare for Murray's martial arts antics in Stranger Things 4.

(135) The character of Eddie Munson was inspired by Damien Echols. Echols was one of three youg men wrongly convicted of three murders in West Memphis. Echols was from a small religious town and the murders were more or less pinned on him because he

had long hair and liked heavy metal music. He actually ended up on death row but became an author after he was released.

(136) The Duffer Brothers got Robert Englund to autograph some Nightmare On Elm Street posters for them when he appeared in Stranger Things 4.

(137) When she auditioned for Stranger Things, Sadie Sink had to do an audition scene with Gaten Matarazzo and Caleb McLaughlin to see if she had any chemistry with them.

(138) Princess Daphne in the game Dragon's Lair is based on Marilyn Monroe.

(139) The horror elements in Stranger Things 4 are much heavier than we've seen in the show before - especially when it comes to Vecna's bone-snapping antics (the bone-snapping was most likely inspired by the film Suspiria). The Duffers said that season four features more undiluted horror because the kids in the show are not little kids anymore and - even more saliently - fans of the show have grown older too. Young fans of the show who watched season three when it came out were three years older by the time season four arrived. This gave the Duffers room to up the ante somewhat when it came to the horror elements in the show.

(140) The missile silo where Eleven regains her powers in season four was designed to look like a real Cold War missile silo. The production designers used declassified military documents to create the look of the set. The set was 300 foot long and deliberately designed to be claustrophobic.

(141) The Michael Myers mask that Max wears in season two during Halloween had to look homemade because you couldn't buy a Michael Myers mask in 1984. The Myers mask in John Carpenter's Halloween is famously a Captain Kirk Start Trek mask spray painted white.

(142) The early designs for Vecna were rather different to how he looked in the end. The first concept art made him appear much paler and covered in sharp shards - rather like a sleeker and ice glazed

version of Doomsday in the Superman comics.

(143) Pennhurst in Stranger Things got its name from Pennhurst Asylum. This was a real facility in Pennsylvania which was exposed in the 1960s by an undercover reporter investigation. The patients there, who were of all ages - including children - were not treated terribly well by all accounts. Pennhurst opened in 1913 and could house nearly 300 patients. It was an isolated asylum with its own power system and security. The fact that the asylum was largely self-sufficient when it came to food also added to the sense of isolation. Pennhurst was finally closed in 1987. There are plans to turn it into a museum. It has become a popular place for ghost hunters to explore in its current derelict state.

(144) Will Byers has a poster for the 1982 stage musical version of The Little Shop of Horrors in Stranger Things 4.

(145) Max's terrible feeling in Dear Billy that she can't cheat fate and is probably doomed owes something to the Final Destination horror franchise. In the Final Destination movies the formula has a group of teenagers escaping from some calamitous accident because of premonition but then dying one by one (in enjoyably elaborate and gruesome accidents) because you can't cheat death.

(146) Note how, at the end of The Dive, Steve Harrington, barefoot and wearing only brownish trousers, is dressed exactly like John McClane in Die Hard.

(147) Dimitri tells Yuri in The Piggyback that he'd heard the double crossing peanut butter smuggler was once a great man who fought the Chinese in battle. This is a reference to the Sino-Soviet border conflict - a seven-month undeclared military conflict between the Soviet Union and China in 1969.

(149) Matt Duffer said that shooting season one was a surreal experience because he couldn't believe that someone had actually let him and his brother make their own television show. It was a dream come true.

(150) Joe Keery is one of the few actors in the show who never

wears a wig to get that 1980s look. He does though have some hair extensions put in at the back because he tends not to have long hair at the back of his head in real life.

(151) Eleven has a poster for the film For the Love of Benji in her bedroom in Stranger Things 4. This is the second in a series of family films about the adventures of a golden mixed breed dog named Benji.

(152) Erica's refrain 'Be kind rewind' was a line that video stores used because it was considered bad sport not to rewind a VHS tape after you'd watched the film.

(153) The overhead shot of Joyce driving Will to the lab for a medical check was designed to mimic the panoramic shots of Jack Nicholson driving his family to the Overlook Hotel at the start of Stanley Kubrick's The Shining.

(154) Polish painter Zdzislaw Beksinski was an important influence on the look of the Upside Down. Beksinski's work was often described as Baroque' or Gothic and featured a number of Doomsady scenarios.

(155) JRR Tolkien was an English author and academic who wrote The Hobbit and The Lord of the Rings. There are many Tolkien references in Stranger Things. One might argue that the kids in Stranger Things are rather like the plucky hobbits in Tolkien's stories and on their own strange and dangerous quest in Hawkins. The boys in Stranger Things use Tolkien's books rather like they use Dungeons & Dragons - to make sense of the bizarre things that are happening. The password to Will's woodland fort is 'Radagast' - the name of a wizard in Lord of the Rings. Mirkwood was a great forest in Middle-earth located in the eastern region of Rhovanion between the Grey Mountains and Gondor. The boys give their quest to find Will this codename in season one.

(156) When Steve shows Nancy how to shotgun beer in Stranger Things this is a nod to John Cusack showing Daphne Zuniga how to do the same thing in Rob Reiner's enjoyable 1985 romantic college comedy The Sure Thing.

(157) Joyce tells Hopper that Murray "is the Starsky to her Hutch" in season four. Starsky & Hutch was a hugely popular cop show with David Soul and Paul Michael Glaser which ran from 1975 to 1979. Glaser later directed The Running Man with Arnold Schwarzenegger which was (loosely) based on a Stephen King (writing as Richard Bachman) novella. In the film version of The Running Man the evil quiz show host is played by Richard Dawson - who hosted the real quiz show Family Feud. You briefly see Family Feud playing on television in Stranger Things 2.

(158) The costume designers on Stranger Things used the 1985 film Just One of the Guys as one of their main reference points for the clothes and fashions of the teenage characters in the show. Just One of the Guys is a teen comedy film directed by Lisa Gottlieb.

(159) The first season of Stranger Things began shooting in November 2015. Little did they know how big the show they were making would turn out to be.

(160) Nancy Wheeler has a calendar for the album Autoamerican by Blondie in her room in season one.

(161) The cast said it actually got quite cold during the season three shoot but as that season was set in July they had to suffer for their art and wear summer costumes.

(162) In season four, Steve refers to Doctor Zhivago being a 'double-tape' at Family Video. This is because the film is well over three hours long.

(163) The name of Eddie's band in Stranger Things 4 is Corroded Coffin.

(164) We see Max watching the short lived television show Misfits of Science in Vecna's Curse. This science fiction comedy series provided an early role for Courteney Cox. It also featured Kevin Peter Hall - a 7 foot tall actor and performer who was later inside the Predator suit in the first two Predator movies.

(165) 'Crop artist' Stan Herd created an Eddie Munson themed crop

circle in 2022 in tribute to the character.

(166) 'Stranger Things: The Experience' - an immersive experience based on the show - opened in a number of cities in 2022. In the experience you get to rescue Max from Vecna and can also visit Family Video and Scoops Ahoy. The experience has drawn positive reviews in the media.

(167) The wigs used by the hairdressing department on Stranger Things sometimes perform 'double duty' and are used by more than one character. Did you know for example that Karen Wheeler and the Lenora Hills school bully Angela both wear the same wig in season four? The wig was just styled differently for each character.

(168) Bridgerton actress Nicola Coughlan said she unsuccessfully auditioned for the part of Robin in Stranger Things 3. Coughlan later (modestly) said that she wouldn't have been as good as Maya Hawke.

(169) It took about an hour to get Jamie Campbell Bower out of his Vecna suit and make-up on the set of Stranger Things 4.

(170) Stranger Things 4 breaks with tradition in that it is the only season of the show where the groups of characters do not all meet up and work together at the end.

(171) Mike Wheeler isn't too convinced by pineapple on pizza in Stranger Things 4. The first person to put pineapple on pizza was said to be Sam Panopoulos. He was a Greek immigrant who moved to Canada in 1954. He created the first Hawaiian pizza at his restaurant.

(172) Stinson, the chief agent of Dr Owens in Stranger Things 4, has the first name Ellen - like Ripley in the Alien franchise.

(173) Family Video was a real company and still had stores open until 2021.

(174) Lucas Sinclair's hair in season four is inspired by rap duo Kid 'n Play.

(175) The Massacre at Hawkins Lab is the first episode where Mike Wheeler does not make an appearance.

(176) In the season four finale, Jonathan asks Will if he remembers the time he got a piece of Lego stuck up his nose as a child. This was actually something that happened to Ross Duffer when he was a kid.

(177) The Stranger Things comics have always been told they can never use the test subject 001 at the Hawkins Lab for a story. This was obviously because the Duffers planned to use the character on the show themselves one day - as we saw in season four.

(178) The Duffer Brothers said the delay caused by the pandemic gave them a chance to go back to their scripts and give them much more detail. One relationship they completely reworked was that of Eddie and Chrissy in episode one of Stranger Things 4. The hiatus gave them a chance to flesh these two characters out much more than they might have done otherwise. This might be why it is a surprise to see Chrissy die so soon. She is so well established that we sort of assume she is going to be a regular character.

(179) Survey company YouGov reported that 10% of UK Netflix subscribers binged the entire second season of Stranger Things in one day.

(180) The designer Aaron Sims says that when they were designing the Demogorgon for season one it didn't have a specific name at that point. It was simply known as the 'monster'.

(181) The director Taika Waititi said he'd planned to use a number of Kate Bush songs in the film Thor: Love and Thunder but abandoned these plans when Stranger Things 4 used Running Up That Hill so famously. Waititi said he didn't want it to seem like he was copying Stranger Things - though he says he is a lifelong Kate Bush fan and claims he had the idea to use her songs before season four of Stranger Things came out. Waititi seemed a bit irritated that Stranger Things 4 had stolen some of his (ahem) thunder and made him change the soundtrack on his film.

(182) Though time is usually in short supply on a production as big

as a season of Stranger Things, the Duffers will usually allow the actors to rehearse a scene a few hours before it is actually shot.

(183) In the crossword that Dr Brenner does at the start of Stranger Things 4, one of the answers is Kali. The clue in the crossword is 'Shiva's wife'.

(184) There has long been a fan theory that the Mind Flayer is really 001 from the Hawkins Lab. Stranger Things 4 more or less proves that this theory was correct all along.

(185) In the show, when an Upside Down scene takes place outside this is mostly done through digital effects (it is obviously impossible to depict a red lightning crackled Upside Down sky or landscape with practical effects) but when an Upside Down scene takes place in an interior or constrictive location like a house then these scenes are usually composed of 95% practical effects.

(186) Eddie Munson was originally going to be more antagonistic and have a rivalry with Steve but they toned all this stuff down in the end and made Eddie more likeable. He's quite abrasive in Stranger Things 4 but essentially decent. We like Eddie - warts and all.

(187) When they shoot an Upside Down scene in the show the production designers float organic pussy willow fluff in the air to get that affect of spores and dust in the environment.

(188) The reason why Millie Bobby Brown couldn't shave her hair off again for Stranger Things 4 is not because she wasn't willing but because she had too many other professional commitments at the time which made this impossible. The makeup department had to study Millie's head shape and hair to make the short haired wig as realistic looking as possible.

(189) Billy Hargrove's licence plate is a reference to the truck driven by Jack Burton in Big Trouble in Little China. Big Trouble in Little China is a 1986 film by John Carpenter. Jack Burton (Kurt Russell), an all-American truck driver with a John Wayne swagger, wins a bet gambling with old friend Wang Chi (Dennis Dun) while in San Francisco. While he waits for his winnings, Jack gives Wang a lift to

the airport where Wang's bride-to-be Miao Yin (Suzee Pai) is due to arrive. However, Miao has green eyes and this has attracted the attention of 2000-year-old sorcerer David Lo Pan (James Hong) who needs a green eyed girl in order to restore his youth and flesh and blood. Lo Pan's gang kidnaps Miao from right under the noses of Jack and Wang and soon the two friends, with the help of friendly sorcerer Egg Shen (Victor Wong), are involved in all manner of mayhem and strange goings on in the heart of Chinatown as they attempt to rescue Miao and Jack's beloved truck - The Pork Chop Express - from Lo Pan's subterranean lair.

(190) The original plan for the Scoops Ahoy costumes was to make them look like pirate costumes but they decided in the end this would be too much of an on the nose reference to
Fast Times at Ridgemont High.

(191) Urethane resins, rope, pool noodles and bubble wrap were used to create the icky vines of the Upside Down in season four.

(192) The sword that Hopper uses in the season four finale to kill the Demogorgon was the same prop sword used by Arnold Schwarzenegger in the film Conan the Barbarian. David Harbour said the sword was very heavy to pick up and wield. Look fast and you'll see that Mike Wheeler has a Conan the Barbarian poster in season four.

(193) Some of the images of Will Byers in the Upside Down in Stranger Things 2 with the snow like ash and dust of this shadow dimension swirling around him seem heavily inspired by similar shots of swirling dusty snow around the boy in the Night Gallery segment Silent Snow, Secret Snow. Silent Snow, Secret Snow is a famous story by Conrad Aitken. In 1971 it was adapted as a segment in the anthology series Rod Serling's Night Gallery - having previously been a 1964 short film. Both were directed by Gene Kearney. Silent Snow, Secret Snow is arguably the best Night Gallery segment of all and a haunting and fragile tale narrated perfectly by Orson Welles. Paul (Radames Pera) is a boy who is becoming increasingly isolated from his parents and the world around him as he retreats into his own inner fantasy life. Paul's secret world is a world of snow. He imagines it sweeping up against the

house each day and whispering to him. The beauty of snow is beyond anything he can imagine and although no one else can see it, to Paul snow is everywhere and all he cares about. His troubled parents bring in a psychiatrist but it appears as if Paul is too far gone now in his imagined world of secret and silent snow.

(194) David Harbour played an inmate in a Russian prison for the film Black Widow around the time that Stranger Things 4 was gearing up. In that film he had a beard and overgrown hair. Harbour suggested to the Duffer Brothers that he should have a shaved head in Stranger Things 4 to visually distance Hopper from the character he played in Black Widow. They agreed that this was a sensible idea. While on the set of Black Widow, Harbour even secretly texted the Duffer Brothers photos of the prison set so that they could make sure the prison Hopper finds himself in Stranger Things 4 would look completely different. Harbour said it was just a very weird coincidence that he had to play two characters stuck in Russian prisons in fairly short order.

(195) Winona Ryder was given the middle name Laura because of her parents' friendship with Laura Huxley - writer Aldous Huxley's wife.

(196) An absolutely pivotal film when it comes to influences on Stranger Things is Poltergeist. Poltergeist is a 1982 supernatural horror film directed by the late great Tobe Hooper. Steven Spielberg wrote and produced the film (although Hooper is the credited director, stories still persist that Steven Spielberg directed parts of Poltergeist). The premise of the film? The Freelings are an ordinary family and seem to have a nice life. Or used to anyway. Their young daughter Carol Anne (Heather O'Rourke) starts talking to the TV, a mild earthquake seems to occur, the TV emits static and strange shapes, things around the house bend and break. And if that wasn't bad enough there's a terrifying tree outside the young son Robie's (Oliver Robins) window. Turns out the house is built on an old cemetery and eccentric medium Tangina Barrons (Zelda Rubenstein) might be the family's best hope. The design of the Wheeler house is based on the house in Poltergeist and in season four the house in California where Joyce lives has an uncanny resemblance to the Freeling house. Static as a connection to otherworld elements is also

a feature of both the film and Stranger Things. The biggest connection of all between Stranger Things and Poltergeist is that Poltergeist, while scary, was actually a PG-13 movie (thanks to lobbying on the part of Steven Spielberg). This is exactly what Stranger Things sought to do. Be scary but still accessible to a wide audience. That mission statement was only really changed in season four - which ups the ante and has horror elements which are decidedly not family friendly.

(197) Another character in pop culture that Vecna's design owes something to is DC Comics Swamp Thing. Swamp Thing - a humanoid/plant elemental creature created by writer Len Wein and artist Berni Wrightson - made his first appearance in 1971. The character (who is rather distinctive as he is essentially a human plant!) allowed the various comic arcs he has featured in to touch on genres like horror and themes such as ecology and corporate greed. Alan Moore's work on Swamp Thing in the eighties remains highly acclaimed.

(198) David Harbour said he treated his Stranger Things audition as a bit of a 'joke' because he didn't think he had any chance of actually landing the part of Hopper.

(199) The Duffer Brothers have formed their own production company and plan to produce a Stranger Things spin-off show. They were rather perturbed though when Finn Wolfhard accurately guessed what this mysterious and top secret spin-off show would be about. "We were on set filming Stranger Things 4," said Finn, "and we were all talking about if there's going to be—like joking, 'oh they're all going to have us back in 20 years and we're all going to fat and old,' that kind of thing. And then I was like, 'But if you guys are actually going to do a spin-off, it should be this.' And then I said it and the Duffers looked at each other and looked at me and they were like, 'Could we talk to you for a second?' And then they pulled me off and they were like, 'That is the idea. Who told you?' and I was like, 'No one,' and they were like 'What do you mean? You just came up with it?' and I was like, 'Well, no, I just thought that that would be a cool way to expand.' It was really funny and they were like 'Okay, well... don't tell anyone.'"

(200) The Duffer Brothers say that Winona Ryder, who was famous herself at a tender age, has been instrumental in helping Millie Bobby Brown cope with the pressures of fame. Few people in entertainment history have gone from relative obscurity to global fame as fast as Millie - and she was only about twelve when it happened. "She's talked to the kids about what celebrity is like and how the press can be and the anxiety and confusion that comes along with celebrity," said the Duffers. "I think she's really helped them. I know she's specifically helped Millie a lot to work through that. And that's something that no one else can help with, really, because so few people have experienced it. It's not something I understand. It's not something that, you know, even a parent would understand."

(201) In 2020 it was announced that a company named Irish Rover Entertainment were taking legal action against Stranger Things for allegedly ripping off one of their unpublished screenplays. The screenplay in question was called Totem and about a girl with powers who has to battle a demon. The 'trump card' that Rover sought to use to their advantage was that Aaron Sims was involved for designs both for them and on Stranger Things. This was not the first time that Stranger Things had been subject to claims that it had copied something but so far these claims have proved vague at best. Lawjournalnewsletters.com reported in 2021 - 'In response to a copyright claim in the U.S. District Court for the Central District of California that the Netflix series Stranger Things infringed on Irish Rover Entertainment's unpublished screenplays, Netflix and the other defendants filed a Rule 12(b)(6) motion to dismiss under the Federal Rules of Civil Procedure, arguing that the works were not substantially similar as a matter of law. In connection with the motion, Netflix submitted — and the district court accepted — copies of the allegedly infringed screenplays and the allegedly infringing three seasons of Stranger Things.

Netflix provided a detailed analysis to demonstrate that the competing works were not "substantially similar" under the "extrinsic similarity" test, which applies at the Rule 12(b)(6) pleading stage. Under this test, a court conducts an objective analysis of similarities between the competing works' plot, themes, dialogue, settings, pacing, characters and sequence of events after filtering out non-protectable similarities (e.g., scenes à faire elements, historical facts and general ideas). In contrast to Irish Rover Entertainment's screenplays — which Netflix described as telling the story of an epileptic army veteran's quest to free his dead wife's spirit from a giant English-speaking angel/demon — Netflix explained that Stranger Things focuses on a group of teenagers dealing with common teenage issues (e.g., conflicts with adults, romantic crushes), while engaging with and fighting off science fiction monsters, evil scientists and Russian military personnel.' It certainly seemed far-fetched that the Duffers would mimic an obscure unpublished screenplay when they already had a billion (Lovecraft, Clive Barker, Spielberg, Stephen King, Wes Craven, John Hughes etc) influences of their own for the show. Besides, it's not as if stories about horror, super-powered kids, and alternate dimensions had never been done before. It is almost impossible to come up with anything completely original these days.

(202) Want some more Stranger Things fan theories that turned out to be untrue? Ok then, be my guest. There was once a theory that Dr Brenner was actually test subject 001 at the Hawkins Lab. This theory therefore proposed that Brenner actually had some sort of special abilities or powers himself (though we hadn't seen them on display in the show). The source of this theory was the fact that Brenner never seemed to be scared of Eleven - despite the fact that she was highly powerful and even dangerous. Could it be that the reason why Brenner was unflinching in the presence of this Jean Grey style super child was the fact that he had similar powers himself? As it turned out, the answer was no. Brenner definitely didn't have super powers in the end and we all know now that he wasn't 001.

(203) Stranger Things (which would have been called Montauk at the time) was initially vague in terms of what format it was going to take. The Duffers thought of it as a movie at first but then decided it should be a miniseries. They then toyed with the idea of making it an anthology in that a second season (should one be granted) would have completely new characters and a new location. Thankfully, none of these things transpired. The anthology format is quite a popular trend in modern television but it does have an element of risk. Take the recent horror show the Terror for example. The first season was incredible but the (completely different) second season

was mediocre at best.

(204) The prison scenes featuring Hopper in season four were designed to have a green fluorescence and plenty of blue to distinguish them visually.

(205) The scripts for the final episodes in season four clocked in at a whopping 115 pages.

(206) A play based on Stranger Things titled Stranger Things: The First Shadow is due in 2023. The new play is written by Stranger Things TV series writer and co-executive producer Kate Trefry and directed by The Crown's Stephen Daldry with co-director Prima Facie's Justin Martin. The play features young versions of Jim Hopper and Bob Newby and is set in 1959. It will also feature the doomed Creel family.

(207) You can now, should you desire, buy some glow in the dark Stranger Things sneakers.

(208) Aside from The Lost Sister, the only two episodes of Stranger Things rated below 8 on IMDB are Suzie, Do You Copy? and The Mall Rats. These two episodes are the opening two chapters of season three - which suggests that fans and viewers perhaps found season three a little slow in getting out of the gate.

(209) Dustin suggests that the Soviets might be dabbling in Promethium in their underground lair in Stranger Things 3. Promethium is the substance used to create Cyborg in DC Comics. In the DC universe, Promethium was first developed by Dayton Labs, a company owned by Steve Dayton. It was a metal named after the Titan Prometheus. He was being punished by Zeus for giving mankind fire and had a giant eagle eat his liver on a daily basis, but since he was a Titan, he grew another by the next day. The metal had regenerative properties which could be used in metallic creations mended themselves, or potentially make highly destructive weapons. In other relativity Promethium can be virtually indestructible depending on continuity.

(210) The mall in Stranger Things 3 is used to reference the classic

1978 George Romero film Dawn of the Dead. Romero shot Dawn inside inside Monroeville Mall in Pennsylvania. Dawn begins in a fictional Pennsylvanian television station. Fran (Gaylen Ross), an employee at the station, wakes from what must have been a bad dream. Reality however is worse than any nightmare. The zombie epidemic is now almost out of control and the television studio is full of chaos and panic as they grimly attempt to broadcast lists of rescue stations that may not even be safe anymore ("We've had old information on the air for the last twelve hours... "). Fran's pilot boyfriend Steve (David Emge) arrives and surreptitiously tells her he plans to steal the network's traffic report helicopter so they can fly out of the city to look for somewhere safer. "Go," says another worker to Fran. "We'll be off air before midnight anyway." Martial law has been imposed and residents are banned from private residences and ordered into central areas of the city. We see a SWAT team attempting to comply with this order by removing the city's poorest elements from a tower block and destroying the undead that have been left.

Most importantly, we meet SWAT officers Peter (Ken Foree) and Roger (Scott H. Reiniger). Roger has secretly arranged to meet up with Steve and Fran to fly out of the city and he invites Peter to tag along. Up in the air, this unlikely quartet survey the carnage of the landscape below. Soon, they are low on fuel and supplies and a huge abandoned shopping mall hovers into view. Dawn of the Dead is a post-apocalyptic satiric horror masterpiece. The heart of the film is the Edenic consumerist environment of the mall - a place that proves rather too tempting to our heroes. Will it be their undoing? The Duffers tap into Dawn of the Dead in a number of scenes during Stranger Things 3. They use the fact that malls become eerie places at night when everyone has gone home (just like Romero did) and the scenes where Jonathan, Nancy, and the kids explore an empty supermarket at night is pure Dawn of the Dead. The moment where Robin slides down a mall escalator is a direct reference to a scene in Dawn of the Dead.

(211) Michael Park, who plays Tom in Stranger Things 3, is another actor on the show with Broadway connections. On stage, he has originated roles in three Broadway musicals - Michael in Smokey Joe's Cafe (1995), Angus Tuck in Tuck Everlasting (2016), and

Larry Murphy in Dear Evan Hansen (2016), as well as Monty in the Off-Broadway production of Violet (1997).

(212) Fast Times at Ridgemont High is a 1982 teen comedy film which has woven its way into the subtext of Stranger Things many times. Steve and Robin's sailor suits at Scoops Ahoy owe much to the Captain Hook Fish & Chip scenes in Fast Times at Ridgemont High. Nancy Wheeler's clothes in season one where inspired by Jennifer Jason Leigh's character in the movie. At the end of season three, Steve encounters a cut-out of Phoebe Cates from Fast Times at Ridgemont High at the video store. A Camaro is destroyed in the movie too and this is the model of car that Billy Hargrove owned in Stranger Things. Steve even makes reference to Fast Times in his first scene in season four when he suggests (not unreasonably you suspect) that its famous Phoebe Cates nudity scene makes it a very freeze framed rental. It transpires that Vickie - Robin's crush - rented this film and left the tape at this exact Phoebe Cates moment. This makes Steve suspect that Vicki is gay - which would be good news for Robin.

(213) In that famous DemoBat concert scene in the season four finale, Joseph Quinn was really playing Metallica's Master of Puppets on the guitar. They only had to edit in a 'hand double' for some of the close-ups.

(214) Eleven's clothes at the start of season four are deliberately mismatched to reflect her confused state of mind. Without her powers and bereft of Hopper and Hawkins, Eleven doesn't really know who she is anymore. The fact that she's living with Joyce too has clearly been an influence. Eleven is designed to look like a mini-Joyce Byers at the start of Stranger Things 4.

(215) Joseph Quinn was 29 years-old when he played high school senior Eddie Munson.

(216) The 1978 remake of Invasion of the Body Snatchers was an inspiration for the organic plant like look of the Demogorgon and Upside Down. This film is also referenced when Will gives a piercing scream and shakes in season two when the scientists burn the tunnels. In the movie, those turned into 'duplicates' by the aliens

emit a terrifying scream when pointing out a human.

(217) In season one, Nancy compares the Demogorgon to a shark in the way that it can apparently detect blood. Is her shark dialogue accurate? Can sharks really detect a single drop of blood in the ocean? From American Musuem & Natural History: 'Sharks are often portrayed as having an almost supernatural sense of smell. However, reports that sharks can smell a single drop of blood in a vast ocean are greatly exaggerated. While some sharks can detect blood at one part per million, that hardly qualifies as the entire ocean. Sharks do, however, have an acute sense of smell and a sensitive olfactory system--much more so than humans. Sharks' nostrils are located on the underside of the snout, and unlike human nostrils, are used solely for smelling and not for breathing. They are lined with specialized cells that comprise the olfactory epithelium. Water flows into the nostrils and dissolved chemicals come into contact with tissue, exciting receptors in the cells. These signals are then transmitted to the brain and are interpreted as smells.

Because of the extreme sensitivity of these cells, as well as the fact that the olfactory bulb of the brain is enlarged, sharks can detect minuscule amounts of certain chemicals. This varies, of course, among different species of sharks and the chemical in question. The lemon shark can detect tuna oil at one part per 25 million - that's equivalent to about 10 drops in an average-sized home swimming pool. Other types of sharks can detect their prey at one part per 10 billion; that's one drop in an Olympic-sized swimming pool! Some sharks can detect these low concentrations of chemicals at prodigious distances - up to several hundred meters (the length of several football fields)—depending on a number of factors, particularly the speed and direction of the water current.'

(218) Before season four came out, Netflix put up a promotional billboard which read 'Protect Steve'. Joe Keery said he rather worried when he saw this because it suggested great danger for the resident Hawkins babysitter hero. There always seems to be apprehension about Steve's fate but it seems unlikely he'd be killed off given the popularity of the character. Joe Keery often feels like the lead of the show at times - which is incredible when you think back to season one.

(219) The shooting location for Forest Hills trailer park in season four was Griffin, Georgia.

(220) When Eleven's life flashes before her eyes when Henry has the upper hand in the rainbow room in The Massacre at Hawkins Lab this seems a lot like a homage to the trippy credits in the original 1978 Superman movie with Christopher Reeve.

(221) Jamie Campbell Bower was simply billed as an orderly named Peter Ballard in the promotion for Stranger Things 4. This was clearly deliberate misdirection.

(222) Netflix had to draft special effects experts from their other shows in order to complete the complex special effects on Stranger Things 4. If they hadn't that we'd probably still be waiting for season four to be released today!

(223) For the death scene of (spoiler alert) Brenner in Stranger Things 4, the Duffers said that Millie Bobby Brown rather amazingly nailed this emotional scene perfectly in only two takes.

(224) If they hadn't got permission to use Running Up That Hill by Kate Bush in season four, Ross Duffer said that the cover of Dear Prudence by Siouxsie and the Banshees was under consideration as an alternative. Another song under consideration was All We Ever Wanted Is Everything by Bauhaus. Both of those songs would have been equally amazing.

(225) There were very vague plans to make Stranger Things as a found footage movie at a very early stage but the Duffers admitted that they didn't actually like found footage movies much so this was a bit of a non starter. At the time the found footage genre was back in fashion thanks to the success of the Paranormal Activity movies. Found footage goes back decades as a subgenre of horror but it was The Blair witch Project which brought it to the mainstream and - for better or worse - inspired the deluge of found footage movies which have been released since 1999. The Blair Witch Project is a low-budget 1999 horror film directed by Daniel Myrick and Eduardo Sanchez. The film had a clever and innovative internet marketing campaign and became a box-office smash through good word of

mouth despite its minuscule budget. The premise is simple and not entirely original. Three students - Heather Donahue, Joshua Leonard, and Michael C Williams - go hiking into the woods of Burkittsville, Maryland in 1994 to investigate and make a documentary film about a local legend known as the Blair Witch. They are never heard from again but the film they shot with their video equipment is recovered. This shaky footage reveals what happened to them in the Black Hills of Burkittsville.

(226) A very obvious movie reference in regard to the incarcerated Victor Creel is The Silence of the Lambs - where the highly dangerous and disturbed Dr. Hannibal Lecter is being held at Baltimore State Hospital for the Criminally Insane. An FBI agent named Clarice Starling must visit Lecter in the hospital in the hope that Lecter might provide some insight into a serial killer who has yet to be captured.

(227) Despite a number of nominations, the cast members of Stranger Things were absent at the 2022 Emmys. It is believed that a combination of other commitments and a sense that they were not frontrunners to pick up many awards explained why no one from the show turned up.

(228) The real location used for the exteriors of Pennhurst Mental Hospital in Stranger Things 4 was Berry College in Atlanta. Berry College is a private liberal arts college in the Mount Berry community adjacent to Rome, Georgia. Pennhurst was first mentioned in the second ever episode The Weirdo On Maple Street. Lucas, lest we forget, idly pondered whether or not Eleven might have escaped from Pennhurst.

(229) Note that Paul Reiser's Dr Owens calls Eleven 'kiddo' in Stranger Things 4. This is what Reiser's character Carter Burke kept calling Ripley in Aliens.

(230) Jonathan Byers suggests a visit to the cinema to watch the comedy film Police Academy 3 in season four but an unenthusiastic Will tells him that the film is supposed to 'suck'. Police Academy 3: Back in Training was released in 1986. There would be four more Police Academy films after this and all but one was released in the

1980s. By the time of the third film the Police Academy formula was starting to wear a bit thin and repeat itself. These movies were very popular though. There was also a short lived Police Academy sitcom and an animated series but both of these have been largely forgotten today.

(231) It would probably be fair to say that the huge success of Stranger Things took the cast and crew by surprise. Most of them didn't even expect to get a second season. Natalia Dyer said that when shooting wrapped on season one the cast said their goodbyes with no expectation that they would be working with one another again.

(232) Jonathan calls the two protection officers guarding them at the Byers house in season four 'Ponch and John'. This is a reference to the two main characters in the police show CHiPs - which ran from 1977 to 1983. The show was about two motorcycle officers of the California Highway Patrol (CHP). Erik Estrada and Larry Wilcox were the leads. Trivia - a supporting cast member was Michael Dorn (later to find fame as Worf in Star Trek: The Next Generation). Bruce Jenner also appeared in the show as a replacement when Erik Estrada had a contract dispute. Bruce Jenner is now Caitlin Jenner. Jenner was a former track and field star who had began an acting career. Do you want even more CHiPs themed trivia? Jenner auditioned to be Superman but lost out to Christopher Reeve.

(233) Look fast and you'll notice that Eddie has a skeleton puppet in Stranger Things 4.

(234) Suzie's house in Stranger Things 4 looks like the one from Home Alone.

(235) Cocoon is one of the films playing at the Starcourt Mall in Stranger Things 3. Cocoon is a 1985 science-fiction fantasy film directed by Ron Howard about a group of elderly people rejuvenated by aliens.

(236) The Flayer particles seem to resurrect the dead monsters in season four. It could be that the Duffers got this idea from the Arch-vile in the Doom video games.

(237) In the scene where Max has visions of her brother Billy in Dear Billy, Sadie Sink shot her contribution to this scene an entire year after Dacre Montgomery!

(238) Vecna's hands contain creepy extra long clawed fingers. Mechanical metal finger extensions were specially built to add to the Vecna suit by the prosthetics team.

(239) The costume department on Stranger Things 2 had a terrible time when it came to finding period authentic shoes because the boys were constantly growing - especially in the foot department.

(240) Believe it or not, you can now buy kitchen sponges made to look like Stranger Things VHS tapes.

(241) You can see a VHS tapes of the films My Fair Lady, Born Free, and Doctor Doolittle in the Byers house in The Monster and the Superhero. The copy of Doctor Doolittle is obviously the version with Rex Harrison.

(242) The Stranger Things writer's room Twitter named Ex Machina as one of the many films which influenced season four. Ex Machina is a 2015 science fiction psychological thriller film written and directed by Alex Garland. Domhnall Gleeson plays Caleb Smith, a computer whizz who works for a famous technology company named Blue Book. Smith wins a competition at his office and the prize is a week with the CEO of Blue Book Nathan Bateman (Oscar Isaac) at Bateman's isolated high tech house in the wilderness. It turns out that Bateman has created an android named Ava (Alicia Vikander) and wants Smith to interview Ava to gauge her consciousness and intelligence. When Ava covers her mechanical looking torso with clothes she resembles a beautiful woman. She soon begins to flirt with Smith and build a rapport. When Smith learns that Nathan intends to wipe the memory of Ava to upgrade her, he becomes sympathetic to this artificial person. Ex Machina is a slick, thoughtful and interesting science fiction thriller with some good central performances - especially Alicia Vikander as the manipulative Ava.

The film's dialogue is a little clunky and pretentious at times

(Garland keeps giving the characters famous scientific quotes to dispense) but this is a very compelling film where the shifting motivations of the characters become very intriguing.

(243) When the titles for season four were released, The Nina Project was (wrongly as it probably turned out) assumed by many to be a reference to a woman named Nina Kulagina. Nina Kulagina served in the Red Army during the Second World War and claimed to have psychic powers. She took part in many experiments in the Soviet Union in order to prove that her powers were real. Sceptics in the West though believe that she was a fraud and her powers were merely tricks and sleight of hand.

(244) The shoot out in the Byers house in Dear Billy was filmed in one continuous camera shot to make it feel more realistic and visceral. The California plot featuring The Byers brothers, Mike, and Argyle is more of an 80s action comedy - as opposed to the horror in Hawkins and Hopper's prison drama.

(245) 2019 saw the release of Stranger Things: The Upside Down Lego set. This 2,300-piece Lego set recreates both the normal and Upside Down versions of the Byers house in Hawkins. Lego Senior Model Designer Justin Ramsden said - "We were really lucky to work closely with Netflix, so they gave us loads of behind the scenes images and plans. You had the TV show out there for everyone to watch and rewatch, so we had plenty of visual goodness showing how they would set up the house in the show, where they would leave a cup on the side when Joyce is talking, or where the cushion goes on the sofa, so really mundane stuff, but that is what I love as a fan, where you get this behind the scene look. We were not shown anything of Season 3 really – which is cool because it leaves it exciting for me, it means I get to build the set in the run-up to the new series and get really hyped for it." A mint condition Stranger Things: The Upside Down Lego set can fetch up to £350 on eBay.

(246) Erica has a poster for the 1982 animated film The Secret of NIMH in her bedroom in Stranger Things 4. This film was based on Robert C. O'Brien's 1971 children's novel, Mrs. Frisby and the Rats of NIMH. The inclusion of this poster is an Easter egg of sorts because the film's director Don Bluth was the man who created the

arcade game Dragon's Lair - which famously features in Stranger Things 2.

(247) The Duffers said the most stressed they have ever been on the show was making the season one finale The Upside Down. Time was not on their side and they had to go without a lot of sleep to get the finale finished. Money was tight too but Netflix did mitigate this somewhat by giving them some extra money for the finale. All the work paid off in the end as The Upside Down is a fittingly epic and emotional conclusion to season one with some memorable moments. The sequence where Eleven violently takes out the government agents in the school corridor remains one of the most legendary setpieces in the show.

(248) The Duffers said that Winona Ryder was rather upset when she learned that Bob Newby was going to perish in Stranger Things 2. Winona was very good friends with Sean Astin and loved having him on the set so she didn't like this plot twist at all. The Duffers did consider keeping Bob Newby alive but in the end they decided he had to go. If no characters in the show ever die then there is no sense of danger and it feels like nothing is at stake. This is why Benny and Barb were killed off early in season one. The Duffers wanted to keep the audience on their toes wondering who might die next. Bob Newby's death was originally going to be more grisly with fountains of blood spewing forth.

Mindful of the fact the show is popular with kids and young teenagers, they decided to tone this down somewhat for fear of being too blood drenched.

(249) Eleven's leg injury in Stranger Things 3 was written into the show after Millie Bobby Brown injured her kneecap in real life when she slipped by a swimming pool. Millie's ability to move normally was restricted at times when they made season three. She had to have a double in the scenes where Eleven rides a bike.

(250) There are many movie costumes at the Halloween party Steve and Nancy attend in Stranger Things 2. These include Rocky, Flashdance, Animal House, and many more. You can also see someone in the Cobra Kai karate uniform of Johnny Lawrence from

The Karate Kid. The Karate Kid was a big hit in 1984 and starred Ralph Macchio as a teenager who is taught karate (and some important life lessons) by the wise and kind Mr Miyagi - the Japanese handyman at his apartment building. There were two more Karate Kid sequels and then in 1994 a reboot (of sorts) with The Next Karate Kid. Mr Miyagi was still around in The Next Karate Kid but Ralph Macchio had been replaced by Hilary Swank. Macchio was in his thirties by now and getting a bit old to be playing a teenager. In recent years the Cobra Kai television show has returned to the Karate Kid universe with great success. Here's some bonus trivia: in The Karate Kid III, Ralph Macchio is supposed to be a high school kid and the villain Thomas Ian Griffith is a Vietnam veteran and millionaire businessman. In real life though, Ralph Macchio is actually older than Thomas Ian Griffith!

(251) Michael Stein still had a day job selling used synthesizers when he was asked to compose the Stranger Things music.

(252) The Duffers described Stranger Things 4 as their 'Game of Thrones' season in that it is more sprawling than previous seasons with the range of locations and larger than usual cast of characters. Despite this though fans seemed to like the Hawkins plot the best in season four. Although the Duffers have tried, with varying degrees of success, to move the show beyond Hawkins to stop it becoming too samey and similar the horror stuff in Hawkins in season four works like gangbusters and feels fresh. The Duffers said that one of the reasons (besides wanting to riff on Spielberg films set near the desert like Poltergeist and E.T) that they had Joyce Byers moving at the end of season three is that it felt unrealistic to them that anyone who went through all this stuff would still want to live in Hawkins. Logic would tell them to get out of town.

This is doubly the case with Joyce Byers because Hawkins has become a place with too many bad memories (not least of which is the late Bob Newby). She also has two kids and Eleven to think about too. It is revealed in season four that Dr Owens was the person who arranged for Joyce to move to California. We can assume that he supplied some financial assistance in the form of getting her a house. Owens' motivation for this was that he wanted to keep tabs on Eleven and so it made sense to have Joyce move out of Hawkins and closer to him.

(253) The Invisibles is a comic book series by Grant Morrison that was published by the Vertigo imprint of DC Comics from 1994 to 2000. In the season two episode titled The Lost Sister, you can see grafitti saying Tom O'Bedlam and King MOB - direct references to The Invisibles. The comic is about a secret society with various magical abilities who battle oppression. Its themes and abstract nature were an influence on the film The Matrix.

(254) You can now, should you desire, buy Stranger Things lipgloss. You can buy literally anything with Stranger Things slapped over the top these days. Yard sprinklers, dog bonnets, chocolate bars, Minecraft, backpacks, candles, hoodies, and so on.

(255) Millie Bobby Brown's real hair is curly though she tends to straighten it in real life. The curly hair that Eleven sports in seasons two and (to a slightly lesser extent) three is Millie's real natural hair. They let her hair go really curly in season two because they wanted Eleven to look like this slightly unkempt girl secretly living in a cabin in the woods with Hopper. Hopper was hardly likely to know anything about hairdressing.

(256) Summer of Night is a 1991 novel by Dan Simmons which the Duffer Brothers have said was an influence on Stranger Things. The story is set in a small town in the 1960s and revolves around a small gang of boys who must battle an evil which awakens. The kids ride bikes and explore the woods, there is a girl who stands up to bullies, and a child goes missing - all components which featured in Stranger Things too. The synopsis of the book is - 'It's the summer of 1960 and in the small town of Elm Haven, Illinois, five twelve-year-old boys are forging the powerful bonds that a lifetime of change will not break. From sunset bike rides to shaded hiding places in the woods, the boys' days are marked by all of the secrets and silences of an idyllic childhood. But amid the sun-drenched cornfields, their loyalty will be pitilessly tested. When a long-silent bell peals in the middle of the night, the townsfolk know it marks the end of their carefree days. From the depths of the Old Central School, a hulking fortress tinged with the mahogany scent of coffins, an invisible evil is rising. Strange and horrifying events begin to overtake everyday

life, spreading terror through the once-peaceful town. Determined to exorcize this ancient plague, Mike, Duane, Dale, Harlen, and Kevin must wage a war of blood against an arcane abomination who owns the night....'

(257) The Duffer Brothers were actually 1990s kids themselves but set the show in the 1980s because that's where all their favourite movies came from.

(258) The exact date when Will Byers went missing in season one is 11.6.1983. There was actually a solar eclipse on this day in real life. The number one song in the United States on this day was Flashdance and the number one song in Britain was Every Breath You Take by The Police. The number one film at the box-office when Will Byers went missing was Superman III.

(259) The Duffer Brothers said they considered pulling The Lost Sister from Stranger Things 2 and simply not showing the episode but decided to include it in the end. They acknowledged that - as fans of the show pointed out - The Lost Sister was a problem when it came to pacing in the season. Just as season two has gone into top gear the handbrake is suddenly applied and we have the atypical detour of The Lost Sister. Not to say that literally everyone hated the episode but, generally, it wasn't well received at all. One imagines that when the Duffer Brothers viewed The Lost Sister they must have realised that, despite its importance in relation to Eleven's personal story, it wasn't exactly vintage Stranger Things and unlikely to have fans on the edge of their seats. Some fans have suggested that, rather than constituting an entire episode, key scenes from The Lost Sister could have been incorporated into a more traditional Stranger Things episode.

(260) DemoDogs pose a different challenge to Demogorgons because they have the ability to hunt in packs and also seem to know how to execute flanking tactics (note how they outflanked Steve at the junkyard in Stranger Things 2). DemoDogs are not as strong as Demogorgons but they do seem to be more agile and might even be faster. All things considered though you'd probably rather take your chances with a DemoDog than a Demogorgon.

(261) Vecna is designed to look like exactly what he is - a human being fused and exposed to the Upside Down to such an extent that he has taken on the attributes of his new nightmarish environment. He's covered in vines and plant like material. Interestingly, the design of Vecna is quite similar to some of the early rejected designs for the Demogorgon in season one. The Demogorgon was going to be covered in tree roots and vines but in the end they made the creature more fungi like and Lovecraftian.

(262) Graveyard Shift is a short story by Stephen King which you'll find in his Night Shift compendium. The story is about workers who have to combat a rat infestation in the bowels of a factory and discover there is a rather large and pesky rodent in their midst. The scenes in the mill with the rats and the Mind Flayer (a 'King Rat' if you will) in Stranger Things 3 feel like a nod to Graveyard Shift. Some of the rats in Graveyard Shift are bat-like - which may have inspired the DemoBats in Stranger Things 4. Graveyard Shift was adapted into a terrible film in 1990. In a 2016 interview with Deadline, Stephen King actually named Graveyard Shift as the worst movie adaptation of one of his stories.

(263) The Demogorgon looks rather like like the plant monster from the video game Empyrion. These monsters are human/plant hybrids and their heads open in a petal flower like way just like the Demogorgon.

(264) A film referenced at the Starcourt cinema in Stranger Things 3 is The Stuff. This is an enjoyable if uneven satirical horror film directed by Larry Cohen. A gloopy white substance that is similar to ice cream is found in a hole in the ground (rather silly the way a man notices the stuff and tastes it, it could be chemical waste for all he knows!) and soon becomes a sensation when sold in supermarkets. Consumers report that it makes them feel great and it also doesn't seem to have any calories. Food manufacturers hire an industrial spy (the great Michael Moriarty) to investigate the 'Stuff' that's putting them out of business. Turns out the Stuff might not be harmless as it seems.

This film has great fun spoofing commercials of the era and gets a lot of juice from Moriarty as the sassy investigator. It transpires that the Stuff, when consumed, seems to take over people, sometimes rendering them violent. The gloopy white substance eats you just as much as you eat it and is very much alive. There are some effective moments of horror in the film but Cohen seems just as concerned with the need to keep the jokes coming. The Stuff is very entertaining but only really derails somewhat when Moriarty gets mixed up with Paul Sorvino as the head of a right-wing militia group living out in the countryside. Sorvino chews up the scenery and these antics topple the film over into too broad a farce. The Stuff was working much better as a satire about corporate greed and how - if there is money to be made - corporations are happy to sell you what they can, whatever the health merits might be. Cohen was particularly influenced by "the sheer volume of junk food we consume every day. We continue to eat these foods despite the fact some of them are killing us. That's when I started thinking that The Stuff could be an imaginary product— in this case an ice cream dessert — that is being consumed by millions and is doing irreparable damage to humanity. Everybody is gobbling down this yummy food, so how can it possibly be wrong for us?"

One could argue that The Stuff might have worked better if it was played straighter with more scares (Cohen believes this is the film the studio wanted) but there's no denying that the offbeat nature gives it most of its charm. The Stuff is a strange mix of comedy and horror but the two leads are good (especially Moriarty) and there's enough clever (ahem) stuff and tension in the story to keep the film ticking over and the audience interested. This is far from perfect but it is well worth watching if you have a weakness for eighties horror films. The Stuff was an influence on the creature effects and duplicate people plot of Stranger Things 3.

(265) So much glue was applied to Dacre Montgomery for Billy's prosthetic wounds in season three that he got stuck to a table while he was having his lunch.

(266) Some horror fans think that Billy Hargrove is rather inspired by Kiefer Sutherland's character in The Lost Boys. Other inspirations for the character are clearly Randall Flagg from Stephen King's The Stand and the eighties Bratpack era Rob Lowe.

(267) Competitive eating champion Joey Chestnut set a record in 2019 when he ate 81 frozen eggo waffles in eight minutes. I'd imagine that's the sort of fact which would give Millie Bobby Brown nightmares! For the record, 81 eggo waffles contain over 20,000 calories.

(268) Millie Bobby Brown said she was a bit worried that people might find Eleven less interesting in Stranger Things 4 because she spends much of the season without her powers.
These fears proved unfounded though because season four provides some of Eleven's most iconic moments in the history of the show.

(269) In the preamble to season four, around the time that a trailer dropped, there was a fan theory that the big bad of the Upside Down would turn out to be a transformed Billy Hargrove. This mistaken theory may have arisen from the fact that Dacre Montgomery was seen in his Billy costume from season three on social media - which obviously indicated Billy was back in some form in season four. It transpired though that this was merely for a cameo in Dear Billy.

(270) Finn Wolfhard said that when they were shooting the first season of Stranger Things he assumed that it would be a show that would fly under the radar and not be seen by many people but then perhaps became a minor cult classic in years to come. He had no idea that the show would enjoy such mainstream success.

(271) Winona is a Sioux Indian name meaning firstborn daughter.

(272) The Duffers said that Stranger Things 4 was inspired (among a great many other things) by The Empire Strikes Back in that the characters almost seem to lose in the end.

(273) In the original early plan for Stranger Things, Steve Harrington was supposed to die in the first season at the hands of the Demogorgon. This is remarkable in hindsight given how popular and important the character became in the show. The Duffers later said that they sort of miscast Joe Keery as a teen villain so decided to refashion him into a different sort of character who would play more to the strengths of Keery. Steve Harrington is a comedic action hero from season two onwards.

(274) Craig Henighan is the sound designer on Stranger Things. The sound design of the Demogorgon took its inspiration from the sound effects that marked the arrival of the Predator in the classic 1987 film. Human and animal noises were distorted and the audio of water dripping was laced in to the give the Demogorgon an icky organic aura. Henighan actually voiced Dustin's Upside Down 'pet' Dart in season two.

(275) Gaten Matarazzo said his agent was furious when he was given the part of Dustin rather than Mike or Lucas (Gaten auditioned for these roles too) because the agent was under the impression that Dustin was a minor comic relief character who would barely feature in the show. These fears were completely mistaken because in later seasons Dustin has more lines than anyone. Gaten clearly bagged a plum role with Dustin. In the early plans for the show the character of Dustin was more of a generic nerd and wasn't fleshed out much. The Duffer Brothers were shrewd enough to allow Gaten Matarazzo to put his own spin on Dustin. Other actors in the show like Finn Wolfhard and Charlie Heaton have seen their lines decrease since season one but Gaten seems to get more and more lines in each season. The Duffers clearly love Dustin and now give him as much dialogue as anyone.

(276) Bob Newby's nickname Bob the Brain is most likely a reference to Bobby "The Brain" Heenan. Heenan was a famous wrestling manager in the 1980s. He was best known for managing Andre the Giant.

(277) It is somewhat ironic that Dr Brenner was the person most qualified to be in charge of the fight against Vecna. Brenner knew more about Henry Creel than anyone. He knew more about Eleven than anyone. He also knew more about the Upside Down than anyone. Brenner was even right when he insisted that Eleven was not ready to fight Vecna. The problem with Brenner though is that his cold logic ignored the fact that Eleven's friends were in imminent danger. Eleven had no choice but to try and help them.

(278) Some video game fans have suggested that the Mind Flayer monster in season three might be based on the necromorphs from Dead Space. Necromorphs are mutated and reanimated corpses,

reshaped into horrific new forms by a recombinant extraterrestrial infection. The resulting creatures are extremely aggressive and will attack any uninfected organism on sight. The Necromorphs are the main antagonists of the Dead Space video game franchise.

(279) The Duffers said that during production on season four they even had dreams about Stranger Things when they went to sleep. Making the show took up an awful lot of headspace - even when they went to bed.

(280) Hopper reveals in season four that when he served in Vietnam he was involved in the preparation of Agent Orange. He therefore believes he was to blame for his daughter Sarah developing cancer and dying. Agent Orange is a herbicide and defoliant chemical which was used by the U.S. military in Vietnam in 'herbicidal' warfare tactics to destroy the jungle cover in which their enemy was hiding. Agent Orange is a known carcinogen. It's safe to say that mixing vats of Agent Orange is a hazardous job that you'd rather avoid given a choice. Hopper says he was just a kid at the time and had no idea what he was doing. The military clearly didn't tell young soldiers much about Agent Orange.

(281) Suzie's sister Eden in season four deliberately resembles Ally Sheedy in The Breakfast Club.

(282) The blue tint that seems to wash over the Hopper arc in season four perfectly captures his mood of sadness, exile, and resignation.

(283) Lt. Colonel Sullivan says in season four that Eleven was apparently being trained by Brenner to be an assassin by means of remote viewing. If that is the case one can see why they were so desperate to recapture her in season one. Someone who had the ability to 'remote kill' from a secure location in another country would be a lethal weapon indeed.

(284) There's an Easter egg at the start of Vecna's Curse when Mike's plane lands. It mimics the orange skied shot of John McClane's plane landing in California at the start of Die Hard. Season three is the one with the most Die Hard references but they obviously resist sneaking a few into season four too.

(285) Chrissy Cunningham's surname feels like a Happy Days reference - though Arnie Cunningham in Christine could make it a double Easter egg.

(286) Suzie uses her computer to help Dustin cheat on his grades in season four. This is a nice riff on similar moments in WarGames and Ferris Bueller's Day Off. Notice that Suzie has a Commodore Amiga. This was a state of the art computer for that era. The Amiga was the more advanced successor to the Commodore 64 - though it would be a shortly sad lived machine. There were some excellent games for the Amiga in its time. By the way, at the end of season one, Will Byers is excited by the prospect of his Christmas present being an Atari system. There was a video game crash at this time which would have made an Atari more affordable.

(287) Some fans of Stranger Things found it rather disappointing that in season four the character of Eleven has been adopted by Joyce Byers and yet Millie Bobby Brown and Winona Ryder barely say a word to each other in the entire season! It would have been nice to see these two actors share at least a couple of scenes. One might argue that Joyce Byers is shuttled off on her comical rescue mission with Murray Bauman a trifle too soon.

(288) David Harbour said that the 'tropical' Tom Selleck as Magnum inspired shirt he wore in season three was chosen by his girlfriend at the time.

(289) Hopper's beer of choice - Schlitz - was created in 1849 in Milwaukee, Wisconsin. Schlitz was once the biggest beer brand in America but they lost customers circa the 1970s after they changed their brewing methods - which some felt made the beer of a poorer quality. The Pabst Brewing Company later bought the company and still produce Schlitz beer today. The brand is still held in affection in the American midwest.

(290) The Craft was mentioned by the writers as one of the influences on Stranger Things 4. This is a 1996 film about four teenage outcast girls who dabble in witchcraft to make themselves more popular and get what they want but, as ever in the horror genre, you should be careful what you wish for. The Craft's central

character Sarah Bailey moves to California at the start of the film and finds it difficult to fit in with the cliques and popularity contests of school and girls of her own age. This theme was an influence on Eleven in California in Stranger Things 4.

(291) The opening scene of Stranger Things 4 is a nod to the 1985 arcade game Paperboy. In the game you play a kid paperboy on his bike who must navigate various obstacles and deliver newspapers to a suburban street. This game was ported to many home gaming systems. If you played video games in the 1980s either in the arcade or at home then there is a good chance that you encountered Paperboy.

(292) Karen Wheeler's hair in Stranger Things 4 is based on Kate Capshaw as Willie in Indiana Jones and the Temple of Doom.

(293) Eddie Munson has some bat tattoos in season four. This rather anticipates his fate.

(294) The production team got lucky when they were looking for a house to double as Mayor Kline's home in season three. They found a house in the Atlanta area that was large and elegant and the sort of place a well heeled politician would live but hadn't had any interior design work done for decades. As a consequence of this it looked like a real house from the 1980s.

(295) At the end of season one, when Joyce, Jonathan and Will sit down to Christmas dinner, notice there are no Christmas lights. For understandable reasons, Joyce doesn't want to ever see some Christmas lights again.

(296) An episode of Stranger Things will usually take about two weeks to shoot. The special effects are another matter entirely though. They take a lot longer than two weeks to complete. In a sense shooting the stuff with the actors is the easiest part of the show from a production point of view. The digital effects though are increasingly complex and time consuming to complete. The Duffers Brothers said they didn't know anything about digital effects when the show started but this wasn't too much of a problem on season one because there were a lot of old school practical effects. This changed

with season two but the Duffers said that Andrew Stanton, who
directed some episodes on Stranger Things 2 and was best known for
Pixar films, actually gave them a sort of crash course in digital
effects and taught them a lot about this necessary field of film and
television.

(297) The Piggyback is the first season finale where Eleven and
Mike do not kiss.

(298) The MK-Ultra project, which features so heavily in season one
of Stranger Things, only became public in 1975 after a congressional
investigation into CIA activities. This top secret operation was
uncovered because someone forgot to shred all of the files. MK-
Ultra was a surprisingly far flung project considering its secrecy.
There is evidence that the CIA conducted MK-Ultra operations in
Canada and even Europe. MK-Ultra experimented with LSD and
basically sought to see if there was any validity to psychics, remote
viewing, and mind powers. Despite the claims of people like Uri
Geller it seems that there wasn't any evidence that any of these
things were real. The psychics you see on television claiming to talk
to dead people are patently frauds just out to make money.

(299) The Roller King in Albuquerque was shut down for a month to
become the 1986 Rink O Mania (where Eleven whacks Angela with
a roller-skate) in Stranger Things 4. The actual location is at 400
Paisano St NE. It's quite rare to have a roller rink still going these
days as they aren't nearly as popular as they used to be in the 1980s.

(300) Sadie Sink said she laughed when she saw Jamie Campbell
Bower in his Vecna suit on the Stranger Things set for the first time.
I'm not sure this is exactly the reaction they were looking for!

(301) The heart to heart between Jonathan and Will in the Surfer
Boy Pizza in The Piggyback was a last minute addition by the
Duffers. They felt like this scene was necessary and that Jonathan
and Will's arc seemed incomplete without it. One could argue that
this is the second season in a row where Charlie Heaton has got
something of a short shrift in the show when it comes to lines. It
appears that The Duffers have rather lost interest in the character of
Jonathan as his contribution seems to have shrunk since the first

season. Natalie Dyer and Sadie Sink, for example, got expanded roles in season four but this wasn't the case for Charlie.

(302) Stranger Things 2 contains the most obscure Easter egg in the history of the show. "When Dustin's on the phone, pretending he's looking for the cat, he's talking to Mr McCorkle," said Matt Duffer. "Mr McCorkle is our neighbor growing up. That's deep cut; you have to live in our neighborhood to know that one."

(303) Nancy Wheeler is a character in Judy Blume's cultish young fiction novel 'Are You There God? It's Me, Margaret'. The Duffers said this was a complete coincidence and that the name Nancy was inspired by the heroine in A Nightmare On Elm Street.

(304) Visual effects expert Aaron Sims worked on Stranger Things and said the classroom showdown in the first season finale between the Demogorgon and the kids was an especially challenging sequence. "The visual effects-heavy scenes were fairly difficult. In the last scene in the schoolroom, where the monster was brightly lit and it had to walk around and look threatening while being hit by rocks - that was all CG. The monster had to be thrown across the room and break apart. That scene was extremely hard for all of us. There was also the amount of time we had to do it - the disadvantage of TV is that the turnaround is so quick. That character was completely CG at that point, so it was very time-consuming. Breaking down the wall in the third episode was also the first time we did a scene that was fully CG. It was a challenge but exciting at the same time; we brought the character life in a unique way, and really showed how it was brought into this world."

(305) Stranger Things didn't get a single nomination at the Golden Globes at the end of 2002. Stranger Things is crowd pleasing popcorn fun so tends to be overlooked at the sniffier end of the awards racket.

(306) According to industry experts, Millie Bobby Brown was the third highest paid female actor in the world in 2022. Only Margot Robbie and Lady Gaga earned more money for acting. This a remarkable position to be in for someone not even out of their teens. Whether or not Millie's career will have longevity remains to be seen

but she clearly has the talent and work ethic to be successful for decades to come.

(307) Ross Duffer said that in an ideal world they would have shot Stranger Things 4 and Stranger Things 5 back to back so it could have just carried on straight on and the younger actors would all have looked exactly the same in both seasons but this was simply not practical. As a consequence of this there will be a time jump between the seasons.

Given that it needed 300 days of shooting and months of post-production to get Stranger Things 4 completed the notion of making two seasons back to back was clearly ludicrous. The digital effects alone would have taken months and months to finish. There is also the fact that the actors have other professional commitments too. It would be impossible to tie down Millie Bobby Brown or David Harbour for two years because these actors are constantly being offered movies. Last but by no means least, shooting two seasons of the show back to back would have placed a preposterous workload on the Duffer Brothers. How would they have found any time to write the scripts for the last season?

(308) You can buy a Magiclux 3D 'Illsuion' Stranger Things Figurine Lamp - which can emit seven different colours. You can choose either Eleven, Eddie Munson, or Dustin as the character depicted in the lamp.

(309) Myles Truitt played Patrick in Stranger Things 4. Patrick is a Hawkins basketball star who has friends, talent, and a good life - until shocking events send his life spiralling out of control. Truitt was best known for his breakout role as Eli Solinski in Kin. He also played Ant in Queen Sugar and Issa Williams on Black Lightning. Myles Truitt had a couple of connections with the Stranger Things cast in that he appeared in the miniseries The New Edition Story - which also included Caleb McLaughlin. He had also been in the TV show Atlanta. This is a show that provided an early credit for Priah Ferguson.

(310) Winona Ryder thinks that luck has played a big part in her career. "For me, half of it has been the sheer luck that I had with Tim

[Burton] and Heathers. Honestly, if it wasn't for Beetlejuice, where would I be? That movie was a big thing for me. Subsequently I think what has kind of worked—and if this is a luxury, I don't know how I was afforded it—but I was not strategic at all. I do remember feeling a lot of pressure. I remember a lot of conversations where I was constantly hearing, You've gotta do this movie so you can do that movie. You've gotta make a big movie so you can make a small movie. But I can't act like that. When I think about the stuff I've turned down or the stuff I wasn't interested in, I don't have any regrets. Yes, there were some movies that went on to be really popular. But now how do they really fit into things? It's very interesting. My whole thing is anti-strategy, and I was constantly being told that I was going to go down in flames for certain decisions. But I am sure that for as many roles that I turned down, there are some that I was never really offered to begin with!"

(311) There is a copy of the bawdy comedy film Bachelor Party on the shelf in the video store in Stranger Things 3. The inclusion of this film is far from random. In fact, its inclusion is a clever meta joke. Paul Reiser was the original star of this film but got the axe because he didn't have any romantic chemistry with the female lead Kelly McGillis (who was also axed). Reiser was replaced by a young largely unknown actor called Tom Hanks.

(312) A band called Greg In Good Company once released a song named Monster's Lair which was inspired by Joyce Byers in Stranger Things.

(313) Cary Elwes is related to John Elwes - who was believed to be the inspiration for Ebenezer Scrooge in A Christmas Carol. John Elwes was a Member of Parliament in Great Britain from 1772 to 1784 and a noted eccentric and miser. Charles Dickens made reference to John Elwes in his last novel, Our Mutual Friend.

(314) Winona Ryder and Maya Hawke have both played Jo March in adaptations of Little Women. Little Women adaptations are obviously based on Louisa May Alcott's 1868-69 two-volume novel of the same title. There have been three versions of this story and all are worth watching

(315) Stranger Things uses the ITC Benguiat typeface for its credits and title. This font was used for the Star Trek films First Contact and Generations. It was also used in the Choose Your Own Adventure series and on Strangeways Here we Come - the last studio album by The Smiths. Quentin Tarantino is fond of this typeface and uses it at the start of his movies for his own writing/directing credit. The recent sleeper hit horror film Barbarian also made use of ITC Benguiat in its promotional art.

(316) D.A.R.Y.L. is a film playing at the Starcourt Mall in Stranger Things 3. This is a 1985 sci-fi fantasy film for children about a family who adopt a little boy but discover he's a sophisticated experiment in artificial intelligence. The government are after him and want to return him to a military facility (where his powers will be of use for espionage and computer hacking). The plot of D.A.R.Y.L. is quite similar to Eleven's arc in season one of Stranger Things. When asked about D.A.R.Y.L. at the time of season one, the Duffers said they had never heard of it. Perhaps this reference in Stranger Things 3 was their way of telling us they know about the film now? The little boy in D.A.R.Y.L. is played by Barret Oliver. Oliver also played Bastian Balthazar Bux in The NeverEnding Story. If you were casting Stranger Things in the 1980s then Barret Oliver would have made a good Will Byers or Mike Wheeler. Oliver stopped acting in 1989 and later became an artist and printer.

(317) Maya Hawke is the daughter of the famous actors Ethan Hawke and Uma Thurman and looks uncannily like her famous mother. There were some (rather mean) assumptions that Maya Hawke only got her part in Stranger Things thanks to some sort of Hollywood nepotism but this wasn't the case at all. Several young actresses tested for the part of Robin Buckley but Maya Hawke was found to have the best chemistry with Joe Keery during audition reads. The fact that she had famous parents was neither here nor there. She was simply the best person for the part.

(318) There seems to be a poster for The Black Cauldron at the Starcourt Mall cinema. The Black Cauldron is a 1985 animated adventure dark fantasy film produced by Walt Disney. It is loosely based on the first two books in The Chronicles of Prydain by Lloyd Alexander. With the budget of $44 million, it was the most

expensive animated film ever made at the time. Earning $21.3 million domestically, it led to a loss for the studio, putting Walt Disney Feature Animation near bankruptcy.

(319) Video game designer and BASIC coder Lance McDonald, in a lengthy Twitter post, defended the scene in The Mind Flayer where Bob puts the lab security back online using BASIC computer code from critics. A lot of geeky nitpickers on the net had claimed this scene was unrealistic. "I was just annoyed at how many people are like 'THIS IS THE DUMBEST SCENE IN STRANGER THINGS YOU CANT RESET A BREAKER WITH BASIC CODE' like as if this was some CSI; Cyber level ****. He's just writing a brute force password retriever on an interpreter that would be on EVERY computer in that era. It's a good scene."

(320) The downtown of Jackson, Georgia is used in the show to double for the town centre of Hawkins. Jackson is in Butts County and has a population of about 5,000. The connection with Stranger Things has been a positive for anyone with a shop or place to eat in Jackson as many fans have visited to look at the locations. When the decision was made not to set the show in Montauk they considered many possible new locations but settled on Georgia as a double for Indiana in the end. Georgia was chosen as the production base because the state had tax incentives which encouraged film production and also good studio facilities. Shows like The Walking Dead were also made in Atlanta - which has led to it being dubbed 'Hollywood East'. What especially appealed to the Stranger Things production designers was that Georgia was very good at depicting the Middle America of a slightly bygone era. This is exactly what they were seeking to do with the show.

(321) Way back in 2017, David Harbour was asked how many seasons Stranger Things should have and was remarkably accurate by suggesting five. "I've heard the Duffers say that they want to end it at four. I will say that I do feel like I would see it run for five seasons. I do know that there's an end to the story. And I know that there's an end for all of these characters. And I'm happy about that, because I don't want it to become like other shows, which are great shows, but like Walking Dead or Game of Thrones where you continue to spiral out of the story just to create content. I know that

we have a story to tell. I know that it can be wrapped up either in four or five seasons. I think four is a little quick. Because I think it's such a great show, I don't want to let it go that soon. But I do think five will be the perfect number where we can tell our story, have it be really rich and something people can watch and go back to watch again. But we can also get out before you get tired of us."

(322) The novel Stranger Things: Suspicious Minds by Gwenda Bond serves as a prequel to the Stranger Things universe. In this tie-in story, encounters with the Upside Down are shown to have happened before Eleven. Suspicious Minds concerns a young Terry Ives and tells the story of how she came to volunteer for LSD experiments under Dr Brenner in 1969 while a student. In the story, a girl named Alice encounters a Demogorgon before the events of season one of Stranger Things.

(323) Heavy metal rockers like Iron Maiden and Venom were used for reference when they were designing Eddie Munson's hair for Stranger Things 4. The hairdressing department said it took quite a long time to get the right wig for the character. Joseph Quinn said he was inspired by the film This is Spinal Tap when it came to finding the right hairstyle for Eddie. This Is Spinal Tap is a comic 1984 mock documentary about an over the hill (and not very bright) British heavy-metal group called 'Spinal Tap' as they attempt to tour the United States for the first time in many years. With a new album called 'Smell The Glove' and a back catalogue of classic songs, including 'Sex Farm' and 'Big Bottom', what can possibly go wrong? The answer is almost everything. As Spinal Tap's tour progresses, they quickly find they are struggling to fill the venues booked for them and that the manager and the lead singer's girlfriend are both competing for control of the group. Battling technical problems, internal tensions, and indifferent audiences, Spinal Tap's tour quickly descends into farce.

Spoofing every rock cliché that you could possibly think of and directed by Rob Reiner (who features in the film as fictional Spinal Tap documentary maker Marty DiBergi), This Is Spinal Tap apparently met with a lukewarm reception upon its initial release. Today the reputation of the film is safely assured as an influential cult favourite. Much of This Is Spinal Tap was improvised by the cast and a vast amount of material was cut down for the film. This is very evident on the 'Special Edition' where the extras include over one hour of new material. Unsurprisingly, the principal cast members who ad libbed much of the film, Christopher Guest (Nigel Tufnel), Michael McKean (David St Hubbins) and Harry Shearer (Derek Smalls), all became familiar comic performers and continued to appear together as Spinal Tap after the film.

(324) The Duffer Brothers have expressed some regret at killing off Grace Van Dien's cheerleader character Chrissy in the first episode of Stranger Things 4. They think that they maybe should have kept her around - especially as she had great chemistry with Joseph Quinn as Eddie. Chrissy is basically used as a device to active the Vecna plot in season four. Chrissy's death introduces us to Vecna and shows us how deadly he is.

(325) The original plan for Stranger Things 2 was for Dr Brenner to come back and play some sort of part in the story but in the end there was no room for him (save for a hallucination cameo in The Lost Sister). Brenner isn't in Stranger Things 3 because the Duffers wanted to have a 'summer popcorn action season' which did not dwell on lab intrigue and Eleven's history. They were clearly saving Brenner's big return for season four in the end.

(326) The Duffer Brothers said that Netflix executives were in tears when they were told what was going to happen in Stranger Things 5. Maybe those tears were because the executives were thinking about the loss of all that revenue from not having any new seasons of Stranger Things anymore! Coming up with a new television show which has global and all ages appeal like Stranger Things is a near mission impossible.

(327) The title The Nina Project references Nina, ou La folle par amour (Nina, or The Woman Crazed with Love) - an opéra-comique in one act by the French composer Nicolas Dalayrac. This music was used in one of the season four teasers. The plot of this opera has a woman named Nina suffering from a diagnosis of psychogenic amnesia after she is led to believe that her lover has been killed in a duel. Nina loses all sense of reason in her troubled state. The Nina Project is the name of a sensory deprivation chamber in season four.

(328) Dustin, Lucas, and Erica use Holly Wheeler's Lite-Brite to communicate with their friends over in the Upside Down in season four. Lite-Brite is a toy invented in 1967. It allows one to design a luminous picture by putting translucent plastic pegs through black paper - the light is blocked by the black paper except where the pegs convey the light. You can buy one of these online if you are curious or want to own one.

(329) Stranger Things 4 actually shows us how Eleven escaped from the lab in season one because we see in 1979 that the orderly 'Peter Ballard' showed Eleven a storm drain exit in the facility. This is what Eleven used to escape in 1983. The exit from that drain must be quite close to Benny's Burgers.

(330) David Harbour said he was grateful that he was in his forties when he became famous through Stranger Things. He said it would have been a lot more difficult to become famous while still a kid - which is what happened to the younger cast members in the show like Millie Bobby Brown. Harbour has said that he does worry that the kids from the show will never quite know what it is like to have a normal life because all they probably remember now is being famous. Finn Wolfhard said that after the show blew up and became a big thing he suffered from anxiety and was once followed home by fans. Millie Bobby Brown now has to have security staff when she goes shopping. You know you must be famous if you can't even buy a loaf of bread without a bodyguard!

(331) Although it is a notable antagonist in Stranger Things 3, in 1985 the Soviet Union only had six years left until it was dissolved. With growing unrest in the national republics, the Soviet Union ended on 26 December 1991, when the USSR itself was voted out of existence by the Supreme Soviet, following the Belavezha Accords. It is somewhat fanciful that the Soviet Union would have had the finances and secret intelligence capabilities to build a secret base under a mall in Indiana - although does at least explain why Dr Owens got fired!

(332) Eleven has spent more time crying than any other character in Stranger Things. There are over twenty episodes where Eleven cries. Luckily for Millie Bobby Brown she's a dab hand at pretending to

cry and finds it easy to do. Millie said that she had to cry during one of her auditions and thinks her ability to turn on the pretend watwerworks might actually have bagged her the part of Eleven.

(333) Production on season four went two months over schedule - which would probably partly explain why fans had to wait so long for it to be released. What with the pandemic hiatus, a range of shooting locations, and billions of digital effects, it is little wonder that we had to wait so long for Stranger Things 4.

(334) The creation of the fair for Stranger Things 3 was a big undertaking. They had to find 1985 period accurate working fairground rides and have them transported in from all around the United States. Hundreds of extras (who all naturally had to have 1985 hairstyles and clothes) were required and the fair had to be designed so that steadicam could be used to follow the characters around. Added to this was the fact that the fair had to have period accurate lights, stalls, and prizes (like Fraggles from Fraggle Rock) and you can see how much work went into the production design. Having the Soviet villain battling Hopper in a fairground is almost certainly an idea that the Duffers got from watching the 2014 thriller film The Guest.

(335) The 'happy place' that Max travels to in her mind to escape from Vecna in Stranger Things 4 is the Snow Ball dance from the season two finale. However, this proves to be unsuccessful and she is found. This is explained by the fact that at the end of season two we saw that the Flayer - an extension of Vecna - was ominously watching over (or under if you prefer) Hawkins as the Snow Ball took place.

(336) In the season four finale, Dustin is plainly dressed like an Ewok from the Star Wars universe. We saw an Ewok cartoon on television in the Byers house earlier in the season.

(337) Steve, Robin, and Nancy are dressed like characters from Red Dawn in the season four finale for their Upside Down mission. Red Dawn is a 1984 film by Jon Milius in which a group of plucky teens - who become known as the Wolverines - become resistance fighters when the Soviet Union invades the United States. The film starred a

pre-Dirty Dancing Patrick Swayze and Jennifer Grey, a pre-Hitcher C Thomas Howell, a pre-Platoon Charlie Sheen, and a pre-Back To The Future Lea Thompson. Red Dawn set a record at the time for having the most amount of 'violent acts' in a movie. The film is sort of like the Brat Pack meets Rambo and not to be taken too seriously.

(338) Sean Astin reached out to the producers for a part in Stranger Things 2. At first the Duffers were quite resistant to the idea of casting him because they didn't want to make it look like the show cast people from famous 1980s movies purely for the sake of it but they were impressed with his audition and sincerity and cast him as Bob Newby after he originally auditioned to play Murray Bauman. Bob was supposed to be killed off in the second episode of season two but Astin's performance was so good that the Duffers decided to keep him around for most of the season and give the character a much more heroic death than was originally planned. Astin was no stranger to being part of a pop culture giant because he was in Peter Jackson's Lord of the Rings trilogy and also The Goonies.

(339) Before the first season of Stranger Things, Joe Keery was told that Steve Harrington would be the school swimming captain in the show and so underwent intensive swimming training prior to shooting. In the end though this was dropped and Steve is not depicted as a swimming ace in season one of Stranger Things. We never saw Steve as a swimming champion in the show but Steve's underwater mission in The Dive confirms that he IS a swimming ace. They shot these scenes in a water tank and Keery and Natalia Dyer had to undergo aquatic training.

(340) Special effects supervisor Martin Pelletier says that the presence of the Mind Flayer in Stranger Things 3 was simulated on the set for the actors in some old-fashioned (but effective) ways. "From episode 2 up to 6, the Mind Flayer was small enough (9 feet tall) that we could use a good old chrome ball as a target for camera and actors to look at. As for the final Starcourt battle sequence, considering the much bigger size of the Mind Flayer (22 feet tall) and the type of action, we did the full sequence in previz as a guide for shooting, and, to make sure the camera operator could aim at something, I used a 30 foot pole with a huge beach ball strapped at the tip as reference for the Mind Flayer's head. Pretty old school but

very efficient!"

(341) Some viewers have suggested an anachronism in Stranger Things to do with road lines. You can see yellow lines in the show but road lines in Indiana were usually white at the time Stranger Things takes place.

(342) The Soviet security men use a Tokarev TT-33 pistol in Stranger Things 3. We also see Nancy pick up this gun and make use of it. This weapon was used by Jennifer Grey in the film Red Dawn. Nancy often has her hair styled in a 1980s Jennifer Grey sort of way so the gun might not be a coincidence. In the 1980s, Jennifer Grey was a successful movie actress well known for films like Ferris Bueller's Day Off, Dirty Dancing and Red Dawn. However, in the early 1990s she did something unfathomable which killed her career stone dead. Grey underwent two rhinoplasty procedures. In simple terms, she had a nose job. After the operations, Grey looked completely different. So now, prospective movie employers were not getting the Jennifer Grey of Dirty Dancing. They were getting a woman who looked nothing like Jennifer Grey! Not surprisingly, Grey's career suffered. She went from being a movie star to obscure TV movies and an appearance on Dancing with the Stars. "I went in the operating theatre a celebrity - and come out anonymous," she said. "It was like being in a witness protection program or being invisible. I remember going to a restaurant where I had been going for years. I ran into people I knew and would say, 'Hey.' Nothing. I'll always be this once-famous actress nobody recognises... because of a nose job."

(343) There is a copy of the 1984 James Garner film Tank on the shelves in the Family Video store at the end of Stranger Things 3. In the film, Garner plays a Sergeant who uses his personal World War II Sherman tank to free his son from a phony drug charge. Tank supplied an early role for C. Thomas Howell - who made his film debut a few years earlier in Spielberg's E.T. the Extra-Terrestrial.

(344) The tradition of Shawn Levy always directing the third and fourth episodes in each season of Stranger Things was more of an accident than anything which was planned. The Duffers were supposed to direct all eight episodes of season one but found that

their workload was impossible because they were still writing the last batch of episodes even when shooting had begun. Shawn Levy offered to step in and direct an episode or two so that the Duffers would have some breathing space to write. Levy, if truth be told, was seen as something of a lightweight journeyman director before Stranger Things - his movies including the family comedy Cheaper By the Dozen and the awful Pink Panther reboot with Steve Martin. He also directed the Night at the Museum films with Ben Stiller. Levy's work on Stranger Things though has been a revelation and he has clearly relished getting out of his family comedy wheelhouse and throwing himself into horror and science fiction.

(345) Millie Bobby Brown's buzzcut wig in season four had to withstand desert sandstorms and a water tank. It's incredible really that it managed to survive all of this!

(346) Stranger Things 4 definitely contradicts and undercuts a lot of the backstory of Dr Brenner's lab from the comics and novels but then you wouldn't imagine that the Duffers were too busy worrying about this as the show obviously takes precedent. It's probably best to think of the show and comics/novels as slightly different entities. While there is clearly an attempt not to clash with the television show (this is why many of the comics and novels are prequels or take place in between seasons) the writers on the comics and novels have no way of knowing what the Duffers are actually going to do in the show.

(347) Matthew Modine is adamant that Brenner is not a villain but just someone who has made a few bad choices. Most fans would probably disagree and think of Brenner as a villain but season four does make him somewhat more complex to judge than season one.

(348) In the eighties it was common and standard for music albums to be released on cassette tapes and Walkmans (a portable cassette player with earphones that allowed you to listen to music wherever you were) were popular. The first Walkman was released in 1979. Cassetes were of course easy to use and record on too. All music lovers in the 1980s would have had a big collection of cassette tapes on their shelf.

(349) Caleb McLaughlin said that because of the pandemic protocols on the production of season four they couldn't film scenes with the extras at first and so had to get all the scenes with only a few characters together in the can first. This meant that scenes were shot out of sequence. So, for example, on a typical day they would shoot something for episode four and then a few hours later shoot a scene for episode seven. Caleb said it was a bit weird to have to do this but they had no choice.

(350) There is an Ethan Hawke Easter egg in Stranger Things 3 when we see a 'coming soon' poster at the Starcourt Mall for Joe Dante's 1985 film Explorers. A very young Ethan Hawke, father of Maya Hawke, played one of the kids in this sci-fi fantasy film by Joe Dante.

(351) A poster on the Family Video window in season four is The Man with One Red Shoe. This is a somewhat forgotten 1985 espionage comedy thriller starring Tom Hanks. The film is a remake of a French film called Le Grand Blond avec une chaussure noire (The Tall Blond Man with One Black Shoe). The presence of Hanks on the window may be a meta nod to the fact he was in Mazes & Monsters - which was inspired by the Satanic Panic concerning Dungeons & dragons.

(352) The building used for the Palace Arcade in season two was a derelict laundry. The Duffers said the building was disgusting when the production team found it. Their renovation transformed it into a 1984 style arcade which was so convincing that locals assumed a retro arcade must have opened in the area.

(353) Theodore and Milton Deutschmann, who created Radio Shack, named the company after the term for a small, wooden structure that housed a ship's radio equipment.

(354) At the Stranger Things 2 premiere, the Hawkins Fair themed party served corn dogs, funnel cakes, fresh donuts, and cocktails such as the UpCider Down, the Maple Bourbon Bone Chiller, and Pumpkin Ale. Half the cast though were still too young to sample the drinks.

(355) When Dustin is playing D&D at the Hellfire Club and says 'Never tell me the odds', he is quoting Han Solo in The Empire Strikes Back.

(356) Stranger Things 4 definitely got a slight backlash from some hardcore lifelong Kate Bush fans. Some of these fans seemed a trifle irritated and snooty about the fact that many young people only became aware of Kate Bush through a popular television show! Kate Bush certainly wasn't complaining though. She seemed very touched and happy that one of her songs had been chosen to play such a pivotal role in the show.

(357) The nightmare imagery Victor is subjected to in the episode Dear Billy somewhat evokes the 1980 horror film The Changeling - which is an interesting haunted house chiller if rather too long (though you do get the always watchable George C. Scott as the lead).

(358) Argyle in Stranger Things 4 is clearly a big fan of Musical Youth. Musical Youth were a reggae band from England who lasted from 1979 to 1985 (they later reformed as a duo). Their biggest hit was Pass the Dutchie - which, appropriately for Argyle, is a song with connotations relating to pot. Pass the Dutchie was the only North American hit the band enjoyed and the song later had a resurgence in popularity in the wake of Stranger Things 4.

(359) Noah Schnapp said that Millie Bobby Brown arranged for a Mariachi band to come in and play on his last day of shooting on Stranger Things 4.

(360) Baskin-Robbins did some Stranger Things themed treats to celebrate the third season. These included Demogorgon Sundaes, the Byers' House Lights Polar Pizza Ice Cream Treat, and the Elevenade Freeze.

(361) Winona Ryder says Sarah Miles's performance in Ryan's Daughter inspired her to become a professional actress.

(362) Stranger Things 3 features the song We'll Meet Again. This is a 1939 song made famous by singer Vera Lynn with music and

lyrics composed and written by Ross Parker and Hughie Charles. It was famously used in Kubrick's Dr Strangelove.

(363) Some music from the movie Killer Klowns from Outer Space can be heard when Eleven makes Dustin's toys come to life at the start of Stranger Things 3. Killer Klowns from Outer Space is a 1988 horror comedy by the Chiodo Brothers about evil aliens who resemble clowns (their spaceship even looks like circus tent!) invading a small town and harvesting people in cotton candy cocoons. The film has become a minor cult classic over the decades - though it is probably a film to avoid if you have a clown phobia.

(364) Mike's longer hair in season four was designed to make it look like he is trying to copy Eddie - who is obviously something of a hero to him at The Hellfire Club.

(365) The Duffers say that working on the television show Wayward Pines under M. Night Shyamalan taught them how to make a television show. Wayward Pines was sort of like a cross between Twin Peaks and Lost. It was certainly watchable but ran out of steam fairly quickly and only ran to two seasons.

(366) Robin's beret in Stranger Things 4 seems like a nod to Jill Valentine in Resident Evil.

(367) The dummy of the 'dead' Will Byers in season one that Hopper cuts into after he breaks into the morgue was constructed by Justin Raleigh. Raleigh's realistic dummies are used by Boston Children's Hospital for surgeons to train with.

(368) When they were writing season one, at the prompting of Netflix, the Duffer Brothers wrote a 25 page mythology of the Upside Down. It was essentially a backstory for this mysterious nether realm. The Duffers say that through the course of the show they have dipped into this essay and incorporated elements - most notably in season four.

(369) It has been speculated that Ted Kaczynski, better known as the Unabomber, was experimented on as part of MK-Ultra when he participated in a series of experiments at Harvard.

(370) If you look really fast at the extras in the Starcourt Mall in Stranger Things 3, you will see a Boy George and a kid who is clearly a fan of Hulk Hogan.

(371) Cary Elwes went to the Harrow school in London. Other famous people who went to this (evidently exclusive) school include Winston Churchill, Benedict Cumberbatch, James Blunt, Richard Curtis, Anthony Trollope, and Edward Fox.

(372) Jason Carver's line to Lucas in Vecna's Curse "First hangover feels like you're gonna split in two..." anticipates Jason's demise in the finale when he is split apart by a molten dimensional lava rip.

(373) Shannon Purser joined the cast of another popular television show in 2017 when she took on the role of Ethel Muggs in Riverdale. A '"Hashtag Justice For Ethel" moment in Riverdale was a sneaky in-joke, referencing 'Justice for Barb'.

(374) When they were hired to compose the music for Stranger Things, one of the first tasks that Kyle Dixon and Michael Stein were given by the Duffers was to pitch demo themes for Eleven and the other child characters in the show. The Duffers knew that Dixon and Stein could do moody and electronic but they need to know that the composers could also do sad and even whimsical too.

(375) In one of the newspaper articles featured in the news clip at the end of Stranger Things 3, the story quotes a 'local man' named Dean Zimmerman. In reality, Dean Zimmerman is the Stranger Things editor.

(376) Adi Tantimedh, who was involved in writing a 90-second fan trailer for Stranger Things in the style of 80s anime, said that - "The way the Upside Down is portrayed throughout the three seasons of Stranger Things is reminiscent of how 'jigoku', Hell or the Underworld, is often portrayed in Japanese movies, folklore and anime."

(377) Robert Englund was born in 1947 and studied classical theatre at acting school. He had early dreams of being a very serious actor. His initial roles were modest and patchy though, including a bit part

in the cult surfing film Big Wednesday and an appearance in Roger Corman's largely forgotten but inventive low-budget Alien clone Galaxy of Terror.

James Cameron worked on the special effects for Galaxy of Terror and actually used it as a blueprint of sorts of Aliens. It was the V mini-series (where Englund played Willie, the kind alien who joined up with the human resistance) though that gave Englund his first experience of real fame. V began life as a mini-series and quickly became a huge phenomenon. It was about a group of aliens arriving on Earth in huge flying saucer type crafts. They appear very human and friendly and establish good relations. It's all a front though. They are lizards wearing human masks and intent on pillaging the Earth and using us as food. The aliens (or 'visitors') are basically the Nazis. They have fascist uniforms and symbols and set up a youth movement. Humans are encouraged to collaborate and spy on trouble makers. V was a huge hit when it first aired and A Nightmare On Elm Street soon followed.

(378) In Numerolgy the number 11 represents the Spiritual Messenger.

(379) Katy Trefery, one of the writers on the show, was used as a stand-in (before the computer effects were added) for the DemoDog in the scene where Bob Newby was killed in Stranger Things 2. She happened to be on the set that day and was the perfect size.

(380) The decision to make Robin gay was not planned in the Stranger Things 3 scripts but evolved as a natural consequence of how season three was unfolding. Maya Hawke and Joe Keery thought it would be too predictable if Robin and Steve ended up as a couple and the Duffers agreed with them.

(381) Sadie Sink said she was originally rejected for the part of Max because she was deemed too old at 14. She begged for a chance to read again though and eventually won them over.

(382) When the third season of Stranger Things came out, the Westworld star Evan Rachel Wood created a mild rumpus on Twitter with the following post - "You should never date a guy like the cop

from Stranger Things. Extreme jealousy and violent rages are not flattering or sexy like TV would have you believe. That is all." Wood seemed to slightly miss the point because David Harbour said they deliberately made Hopper grouchy and insecure in season three so as to make his 'Gandalf the White' rebirth in season four more effective.

(383) When they designed the sound for the Upside Down in the show the sound designers used recordings of trees creaking in the forest in order to get that discordant and strange background aura.

(384) Gaten Materazzo said that on Stranger Things the cast is usually not allowed to view any scripts until they arrive in Atlanta to begin production. Sometimes they only get a few scripts at a time so have no idea what is going to happen at the end (until they actually shoot it of course). The purpose of all of this is - of course - to avoid spoilers leaking. The Duffers clearly trust no one - not even the cast!

(385) Senior VFX producer Christina Graff says it was tricky to make Dart 'cute' in Stranger Things 2 as Demogorgons have no eyes and so appear naturally sinister and alien. They had to make the creature appealing through body language.

(386) Stranger Things 3 wasn't the first time that Limahl had experienced a fresh wave of interest in one of his old songs. The 2018 interactive episode of the anthology show Black Mirror titled Bandersnatch used the 1983 song Too Shy by (Limahl's band) Kajagoogoo.

(387) In the 1983 set season one of Stranger Things it is implied that Joyce is prescribed Prozac but this antidepressant wasn't available until 1987.

(388) Invitation to Hell is a TV movie horror thriller directed by Wes Craven. In the film Robert Urich plays Matt Winslow, a mild mannered scientist who moves into a wealthy suburb to take up a fancy new job with a corporation. Matt is joined by wife Pat (Joanna Cassidy) and kids Robert (Barret Oliver) and Chrissy (Soleil Moon Frye). He's designing a new type of spacesuit which can withstand extreme temperatures (apparently a space mission to Venus is due to

occur in the next three years!) and settles into his new position at the corporation. The transition is helped by the presence of Matt's old friend Tom (Joe Regalbuto) who already works at the company and lives in the area with his family. However, Matt starts to notice that everyone in the community seems to be a member of Steaming Springs - a country club in the area. Matt finds himself coming under increasing pressure from everyone to join the club but he resists these demands and grows increasingly suspicious of the vampish Jessica Jones (Susan Lucci) - the woman who seems to run Steaming Springs. Invitation to Hell has some obvious satirical qualities and offers a pointed critique on snobbery and the need people feel to move up in the world in the eyes of their friends. Characters in the film are shown to be ludicrously excited about new furniture, expensive cars, living in a big house and - of course - becoming a member of an exclusive country club. Matt's resistance to these luxuries is what may ultimately protect him from harm. The dangers of conformity here make the film feel like a blood relative to The Stepford Wives (and its attendant and mostly awful TV sequels) - a film which amusingly played on this concept and offered horror lurking beneath the surface of deep suburbia. Invitation to Hell effectively draws a diabolical net around Matt and although the film becomes rather preposterous in the third act it's always very watchable and fun at times.

You just know that this experimental spacesuit is going to be deployed at some point. The main intrigue comes from Matt discovering the door to what seems to be an underground sauna in the basement of the club. It is through this door that new members must enter as part of a ceremony. You can probably guess what this represents but it invokes a great curiosity in the viewer all the same. Invitation to Hell makes you think of Stranger Things when Matt dons his spacesuit and explores the strange other dimension on the other side of the sauna. These scenes are quite reminiscent of Hopper and Joyce in the hazmat suits venturing into the Upside Down for the finale of season one of Stranger Things. Here's another connection too - the actress that Eleven impersonates while watching all My Children on television in Hopper's cabin in season two is Invitation to Hell star Susan Lucci. Want more connections between this movie and Stranger Things? Well, Invitation to Hell also features Barret Oliver of The NeverEnding Story and Soleil Moon Frye. Soleil

Moon Frye was in the kids sitcom Punky Brewster - a show we see playing on television in The Lost Sister.

(389) To voice Joyce Byers in foreign language versions of Stranger Things, Netflix hired some of the same foreign voice actors who had dubbed Winona Ryder in films like Edward Scissorhands, Bram Stoker's Dracula, and Beetlejuice.

(390) Scientists think that the use of Planck's constant in Stranger Things 3 contained a mistake. Suzie recites Planck's constant as 6.62607004 (without the units that come after it). Scientists at the National Institute of Standards and Technology noticed that this is the value established for Planck's constant in 2014. In 1985, when the show is set, it would have been the value established in 1973, which is 6.626176* 10^-34.

(391) During the press interviews for Stranger Things 2, the Duffers suggested that Kali would be back in the third season. They must have changed their minds at some point because Kali did not appear in Stranger Things 3. It feels like the Duffers were quite burned by the negative critical reception to The Lost Sister and this seemed to put them off featuring Kali again.

(392) The Stranger Things 4 finale marks Dustin's first visit to the Upside Down. It was definitely a trip that Dustin would prefer to forget.

(393) The Palace Arcade has the following games - Dragon's Lair, Dig-Dug, Asteroids, Galaga, Centipede and Pac-Man. You also see a game called Quest for the Space Knife but this is a fictitious game and a joke reference to one of the production crew of Stranger Things having a music group called Space Knife. If you look fast you'll also see a poster for a movie called Quest for the Space Knife in the cinema lobby in season two.

(394) The place where Jason Carver's basketball gang crash and hang out in season four is the now boarded up Benny's Burgers from season one.

(395) The look of Vickie (Amybeth McNulty) in Stranger Things 4

is based on eighties icon Molly Ringwald. The hairdressing department on the show actually had some contact with Molly Ringwald to help get Vickie's hair the right colour. They even got hold of a prop hat that Molly Ringwald had once worn.

(396) Matthew Modine, who like Sadie Sink is a vegan, says he can bake a mean apple pie. "I use Granny Smith apples because they're sour and I don't ever put sugar in my pies. I mix other fruit like mangoes with the apples and that takes care of the sweetness."

(397) "Gathered together by Professor Charles Xavier to protect a world that fears and hates them, the X-Men had fought many battles, been on adventures that spanned galaxies, grappled enemies of limitless might, but none of this could prepare them for the most shocking struggle they would ever face. One of their own members, Jean Grey, has gained power beyond all comprehension, and that power has corrupted her absolutely! Now they must decide if the life of the woman they cherish is worth the existence of the entire universe!" The Dark Phoenix Saga is surely the inspiration for the moment in The Gate when Eleven goes full on Dark Phoenix to close the portal to the Upside Down. We can perhaps say that Jane Ives is a real life Jean Grey but - thankfully - in control of her powers.

(398) To celebrate Halloween Horror Nights, Universal Studios Hollywood whipped up a number of Stranger Things themed dishes in 2019. These included a Demo-Dog (a hot dog topped with beef chili, cheddar cheese sauce, crushed Flamin' Hot Cheetos with sour cream and scallions, served with a side of tater tots), The Upside Down Burger (topped with cheddar cheese sauce and Flamin' Hot Cheetos), and the Demogorgon's Totcho - tater tots covered in in spicy queso, chili, Flamin' Hot Cheetos, sour cream, and scallions. Anyone who had room for dessert could also enjoy Eleven's Waffle Sundae - which had mini waffles and vanilla ice cream covered in strawberry sauce, jelly beans, chocolate chips and Reese's Pieces.

(399) There is a copy of Mad Max in the Family Video store in season three. Mad Max is a 1979 Australian dystopian action thriller film directed by George Miller and featured a young Mel Gibson. This film inspired the title of the opening episode of season two.

Mad Max got a (fantastic) sequel in 1981 with Mad Max 2 (aka The Road Warrior). Stranger Things 3 is set a mere week before the release of the third film - Mad Max Beyond Thunderdome. In 2015, the character returned in George Miller's excellent Mad Max: Fury Road with Tom Hardy replacing Mel Gibson. It was Charlize Theron's short hair in Mad Max: Fury Road that helped to persuade Millie Bobby Brown to have her head shaved to play Eleven in season one of Stranger Things.

(400) In 2016, the BBC website, in relation to parallel dimensions and universes, wrote - 'Is our Universe one of many? The idea of parallel universes, once consigned to science fiction, is now becoming respectable among scientists – at least, among physicists, who have a tendency to push ideas to the limits of what is conceivable. In fact there are almost too many other potential universes. Physicists have proposed several candidate forms of "multiverse", each made possible by a different aspect of the laws of physics. In at least some of these alternative universes, it has been suggested, we have doppelgängers living lives much like – perhaps almost identical to – our own. That idea tickles our ego and awakens our fantasies, which is doubtless why the multiverse theories, however far-out they seem, enjoy so much popularity.'

(401) A surprisingly important influence on Stranger Things was the 1983 John Carpenter film Christine - which was based on a story by Stephen King. In the film, wimpy, put upon teenage nerd Arnie Cunningham (Keith Gordon) purchases an old red-and-white 1958 Plymouth Fury car nicknamed "Christine" and lovingly begins to restore it. But ownership of the car seems to distort Arnie's personality over time. He becomes aloof and arrogant, the opposite of his former self. When a group of school bullies attempt to wreck Christine, the car seems to repair itself in ghostly fashion and - with Arnie behind the wheel - is soon out for revenge. What are the parallels between Christine and Stranger Things and why are they important? It's not so much the premise but more the whole look and atmosphere of Christine that seems to anticipate Stranger Things. Although set in the late seventies, Christine was released in 1983, the same year that Stranger Things is set (the first season at least). The costumes, film grain, props, school corridors, and teenagers in Stranger Things all seem as if they've been partly patterned on

Christine. They have a very similar look and aura. One could say too that Barb is rather like Arnie - at least the Arnie at the start of the story. Socially shy and reliant on her friendship with Nancy for any social status she might have. In the same way that Arnie is reliant on Dennis.

(402) Jamie Campbell Bower said that Millie Bobby Brown was a bit tearful and overwhelmed when she had to do close up scenes with Vecna in season four.

(403) The film that the kids sneak in to watch at the mall cinema in the first episode of season three is Day of the Dead - the final part George Romero's legendary zombie trilogy after Night of the Living Dead and Dawn of the Dead. Day of the Dead is set in an underground army missile bunker near the Florida Everglades (a 25-acre limestone mine in Pennsylvania was used for the shoot). A small group of scientists and soldiers are trapped there in an uneasy and fractious alliance - their dwindling numbers depleted by death and their despairing sense of isolation compounded by the fact that they can't contact anyone on the radio now, not even Washington. Dr Logan (Richard Liberty) speculates that the dead now outnumber the living by 400,000 to 1. It would bad enough if you were outnumbered by pedantic people by 400,000 to 1 but flesh eating zombies! In an ironic reversal of their traditional roles, the living are underground while the dead wander around on the surface, now the masters of what used to be civilisation.

The last film in Romero's classic original trilogy, Day was generally considered to be the weakest of the three but has gained in stature in the years since its release and Romero has suggested it was his own personal favourite. It was originally intended to be an epic set on an island where some zombies had been brought under control. The original draft had helicopters flying into battle against zombies playing Amazing Grace on the PA system but this was all drastically changed when Romero refused to compromise on the rating the film would have and therefore failed to get $7.5 million required to bring his vision to life. The end result is a compromise but still an interesting and solid end to the trilogy. It's the darkest film in the saga (and the most gore laden) and has a remarkably claustrophobic and strange atmosphere. The start of Day Of The Dead (as seen in

Stranger Things 3) with the heroine experiencing a nightmare is superb. A helicopter (to the strains of John Harrison's enjoyably dated and very eighties score) then lands in the deserted streets of Miami. Sarah (Lori Cardelle), one of the scientists and our lead heroine, and soldier Miguel (Anthony Dileo Jr), climb out and use a loudspeaker to try and summon any survivors ("HELLO! Is anyone there?") but the only response is the unsettling moan of thousands of zombies.

Cletus Anderson's wonderful matte paintings are used effectively here to portray this atmosphere of civilisation blown to the winds. The living dead begin to shuffle out of the shadows and lurch towards the helicopter (the make-up for them is more realistic and grungy than it was in Dawn) and an old newspaper flutters in the breeze until it comes to a halt to reveal the headline - The Dead Walk! It's a brilliant intro and nothing else in the film can ever quite live up to it. Day has little of the humour of Dawn and is the bleakest of the three films. This sense is heightened by the gloomy location. Zombies are kept in a corral in the mine for the scientists to study and it's very creepy when we are first shown this area. The white corridors and rooms of the complex seem foreboding and constrictive too with flickering lights and a general sense of dread. The acting is very ripe in Day of the Dead and the psychopathic soldier characters in particular are rather broad, one dimensional and unbelievable. You can't help though but enjoy the preposterous scenery chewing theatrics of Joseph Pilato as our villain Captain Rhodes.

The best performances in the film are supplied by Richard Liberty as Dr Logan, and Sherman Howard as Bub, a zombie Logan is trying to "domesticate". We soon realise that Logan is completely bonkers and he has some good verbal jousts with Rhodes in the film. I'm not a huge fan of making zombies too sympathetic (this got out of hand in Romero's Land of the Dead) but Sherman - a former mime artist - is fine as Bub, a zombie who begins to recover microscopic fragments of humanity when Logan teaches him tricks and brings him artifacts like books, music and razors to try and jog any residual memories that might be there. Two characters that are probably needed at times in what is a grim film are John (Terry Alexander) McDermott (Jarlaith Conroy) - a West Indian helicopter pilot and

Irish radio operator. These seem to be the only two sane people in the complex apart from Sarah and live in a caravan away from the others. John believes they should steal the helicopter and find an island somewhere in the sun. One of the best scenes in the film occurs when Sarah visits their caravan and John shares his take on their situation. "This is a great, big, 14 mile tombstone! With an epitaph on it that nobody gonna bother to read." Neither Cardelle, Alexander or Conroy are likely to have too many memories of quaffing champagne at the Oscars and waiting with great anticipation to see if their name is contained within the envelope but their characters are likeable and it's important in a dark film like this to have someone to root for. Jon Amplas, the star of Romero's brilliant vampire film Martin, also has a smallish role as one of the beleaguered scientists. Day of the Dead is enriched by its doom laden atmosphere and builds to an enjoyably blood drenched finale. Be warned that this is the nastiest of the three films and Romero spares you no detail when the flesh munching capers arrive. Strong stomachs will be needed at times.

It's rather talky compared to Dawn though and the slow pace might be a drawback to some viewers. Day of the Dead is a meditation on how human beings so often fail to communicate and resolve problems. It's about not getting on at any level and the problems that arise from this. The world as we know it may have ended but petty human disputes and egos still exist. Day of the Dead is different enough from the others to stand on its own feet but still feels like a (ahem) blood relative of the first two films (in a manner that the later Land of the Dead probably doesn't). Day of the Dead certainly has its moments and is a fine way to end the trilogy. Day of the Dead hadn't actually come out when the start of Stranger Things 3 takes place so we have to assume that Starcourt arranged a preview screening (though it seems rather unlikely that a mall cinema would be screening an unrated low-budget horror movie).

(404) Vicki Howard, a Lecturer in History and author of the book From Main Street to Mall: The Rise and Fall of the American Department Store, says she was very impressed by the authenticity of the Starcourt Mall teaser trailer for Stranger Things 3. "I looked at the trailer and I couldn't tell if it was an actual clip of a real promotion or if it was fictionalized, and I've seen a lot of these, so it

looked highly accurate to me. Even the music and the way they promoted the mall as this upbeat, sort of cheerful, idealistic vision of shopping. It was fictional, right? I couldn't even tell and I'm an expert on that!"

(405) In October 2020, in a piece of mischief, the Stranger Things writer's room released some titles for the new season four episodes which were less than serious. They included Wakey Wakey Eggs and Bakey and You Snooze You Lose. Fans could sleep easy that these were not the real titles.

(406) Breaking Away is a cult 1979 film directed by Peter Yates. This film was an unlikely but clear influence on Stranger Things with its Indiana setting, quarry scenes, and love of bicycles. The story revolves around four working-class teenagers, Dave (Dennis Christopher), Mike (Dennis Quaid), Cyril (Daniel Stern) and Moocher (Jackie Earle Haley), from Bloomington, Indiana, who have left school but don't know what to do with their lives and spend lazy summer days hanging around and swimming in an abandoned limestone quarry. The boys are known as 'cutters' by the rich kids at nearby Indiana University due to Bloomington´s stone cutting history and are generally looked down upon as losers by the students they encounter. Mike is an aimless out of shape former school quarterback while Moocher has fallen in love but can't even afford a marriage license. Cyril is tall and clumsy and expected to fail while Dave worships all things Italian through his love of cycling and now speaks in an Italian accent, much to the exasperation of his blue collar car salesman father Ray (Paul Dooley). When they ask Dave to form a cycling team to enter the Indiana University Little 500 bicycle race, the boys finally have a chance to make their mark on the town and life.

Nominated for five Academy Awards, Breaking Away is a very charming and uplifting coming of age film about making choices and trying to work out who you are. The film is both an interesting drama and a crowd pleaser with some very funny moments and has a languid summer atmosphere generated by the numerous scenes of the boys lazily lounging around the quarry talking nonsense. The famous central character in Breaking Away is Dave Stoller and Dennis Christopher gives a very natural, sensitive, and appealing performance in the film. Like Bud Cort in Harold & Maude, you couldn't imagine anyone else playing Dave Stoller after watching Breaking Away. Whether shaving his legs in the bath ("Certo! All the Italians do it!") or singing along to his Italian opera records, Christopher gives a memorable performance and his interaction with his mother and father in the film is wonderful at times. "Since you won that Italian bike, man, you've been acting weird," says Moocher of Dave, who has even renamed the family cat Fellini. There are some lovely images and moments in Breaking Away like Stoller racing along busy roads in the slipstream of a truck or gliding down hazy country lanes on his cycle. The scenes in the quarry with the sun glinting off the water are great too and the location is also used for quite a tense swimming duel between Mike and one of the rich kids. You can't help but love too the bit where Dave furiously pedals away on a rooted bike at his father's car dealership in the rain to prepare for a race. Another sequence where Dave races a professional Italian bicycling team is hugely enjoyable as he attempts to banter with them as they rattle around country roads, the Italians not quite sure what to make of him! The town and campus scenes are very authentic in Breaking Away. You get a real sense of a town where the young alienated locals feel somewhat sad when they contrast their own lot and prospects with that of the ambitious students who live in their midst.

The fact that this seems like a real place rather than some sort of Spielberg 'Hollywood' town makes Breaking Away feel like a real slice of small town Americana. Because they are dismissed as local 'cutters', we sense that the boys confidence is such that they don't think they are capable of being anything else. "We rednecks are few, college paleface students are many," says Cyril. Dennis Quaid's character comments that the school's quarterback will be new and young each year while he grows ever more out of condition and farther away from his youthful dreams. Despite the occasional bittersweet nature of the film though, Breaking Away is ultimately an uplifting and enjoyable story where you come to like the characters and hope everything works out alright for them. Ray Dooley has brilliant comic timing as Dave's increasingly bewildered father ("I'm not papa. I'm your god-damned father!") and the scenes between him and Christopher are a delight. There is a wonderful sequence in the film where Dave works at the car dealership for a brief spell and proves far too naive and romantic to survive in the real world, or in this case, hustle cars to customers. The look on Dooley's face as Dave tells a customer "We are poor but we are honest" is priceless. "I had a dream last night," says Dooley. "That everyone I ever sold a car to came back and there you were, handing them back their money!" Their relationship has a real arc and is quite touching in places, particularly a moment when Dave overhears his father talking about him in bed late at night and starts crying. One of the best scenes comes later in the film when Dave and his father walk around the quiet town centre at night and talk about Dave applying for university, being a 'cutter', and the quarries, where Dave's father used to work but now, due to industrial decline, serve as a makeshift swimming pool for local kids with too much time on their hands. "I was proud of my work. And the buildings went up. When they were finished the damnedest thing happened. It was like the buildings were too good for us. Nobody told us that." Barbara Barrie is memorable in the film also as Dave's mother, the parent more willing to indulge his retreat into fantasy until he works out what he wants to do. All the cast have their moments in the film and come across as interesting, human characters. Dennis Quaid conveys a real sense of frustration as Mike ("They're gonna keep calling us cutters. To them, it's just a dirty word. To me, it's just something else I never got a chance to be...") and Daniel Stern is gangly and wisecracking as Cyril, who has some good lines in the film - "I wouldn't mind thinking I was someone myself."

Cyril's jokes hide his own insecurities but he has some funny moments, including a bit where he gets a bowling ball stuck to his hand in a scuffle with the rich kids. Jackie Earle Haley, now famous for playing Rorschach in Watchmen, was, oddly enough, a David Cassidy type heart-throb in the seventies and Moocher has a romance with Amy Wright as Nancy in the film which is touching given their lack of money and prospects. Haley is also given a nice bit where he lands a job as a general dogsbody in a garage and lasts about twenty seconds. I suppose you could say the film becomes more conventional for the cycle race climax but you are emotionally invested in the characters by this point and find it easy enough to get into the spirit of the race - which is certainly well staged by Peter Yates. You want these characters to have a victory of some sorts in life and boost their self esteem so they can move on. There is a sweet subplot in the film too where Dave woos University student Kathy (Robyn Douglass), who, naturally, thinks he's a real Italian on an exchange visit! A pleasant sequence involves Dave sneaking onto the campus at night to serenade Kathy outside her dorm bedroom. The film has a very satisfying resolution and ends on an amusing note with a great final line from Christopher to Dooley. Breaking Away is just a very charming and enjoyable film with great characters and performances and an uplifting quality. I wonder if Eleven calling Brenner "Papa" was inspired by Dave Stoller? In the third season of Stranger Things, Lucas even wears a cycling cap which is an explicit nod to Breaking Away.

(407) Millie Bobby Brown had no idea in her Stranger Things auditions that Eleven was going to have special super powers nor that she would be playing a major character in the show. Millie would later say she had assumed Eleven was going to be a minor sidekick who wouldn't be in the show very much. Millie's auditions for Stranger Things were made up of special scenes created solely for her screen tests. Millie said she had to do several auditions for the part of Eleven. In the end she was flown to Los Angeles for more screen tests. At this point she realised that she must be quite close to getting the part if they were taking all the time and expense to fly her across the Atlantic. The Duffer Brothers said that around 300 girls read for the part of Eleven before Millie Bobby Brown was cast in the role.

(408) Gaten Matarazzo pointed out that one of the worst things about Eddie Munson's death was the fact that Dustin would probably have had no choice but to leave the body in the Upside Down - where it most likely would have been eaten by bats. This is what you could call an example of 'fridge horror' - which is something in a film or television show which becomes more disturbing in hindsight that more you think about it afterwards. It would have been impossible for the injured Dustin to get Eddie's body back and through the portal. Besides, given that the authorities, media, and people of Hawkins thought that Eddie was a Devil worshipping serial killer maniac what would they have done with the body? It would have been difficult to give him a dignified funeral. Gaten said that thinking about all of this must have taken a heavy toll on Dustin.

(409) The acronym for Hawkins Power and Light, the cover name
for the secret government agency experimenting with the Upside
Down in season one, is HPL. This is a reference to the H.P.
Lovecraft. Lovecraft's stories are often about inexplicable creatures,
unimaginable horrors, alternate dimensions, and dark forces we can't
possibly understand. His work was a big influence on Stranger
Things. The Upside Down is what you could describe as
Lovecraftian in that it is very difficult to understand.

(410) It was noticeable that several of the films referenced on the
writer's room board in relation to Stranger Things 4 had
nightmare/dream or virtual reality imagery. The films referenced
included Altered States, What Dreams May Come, Bill and Ted's
Bogus Journey, The Matrix, The Cell, and Scrooged. A slightly
obscure but interesting film referenced was the 1995 cyber thriller
Hackers. In this film a bunch of computer hacking teenagers take on
a villain who surfs through the net. Hackers is laughably dated but
quite good fun. It is probably most notable for providing Angelina
Jolie with an early role. Though the film is a bit silly you can clearly
see that Jolie has star potential and is destined for better things.

(411) In the scene in Stranger Things 4 where Hopper has his head
shaved in the Russian prison this was done for real - meaning that
they only had once chance to do the scene and had to do it
satisfactorily in one take. Thankfully, they managed to achieve this.

(412) The mindscape nightmare sequences in Stranger Things 4
were influenced by a number of movies. One of these was
Constantine - a 2005 film directed by Francis Lawrence with a
screenplay by Kevin Brodbin and Frank Cappello. The film is based
on Vertigo Comics' Hellblazer comic book, with plot elements taken
from the "Dangerous Habits" story arc (issues #41–46) and the
"Original Sins" story arc. John Constantine was created by Alan
Moore and Stephen R. Bissette, and first appeared as a supporting
character in The Saga of the Swamp Thing #37 (June 1985).
Constantine was not a huge financial success and met with a mixed
critical reception. Time seems to have been relatively kind to the
film now and it's picked up a modest cult following over the years.
The main difference between the comics and the film is that the
streetwise British magician is now an American gumshoe who deals

with the occult. It's best just to regard this film as it's own thing as the name of the character aside it's not too faithful to the comics.

(413) Trying to decipher the episode titles and work what they mean in the context of the actual episodes is a long established pastime for Stranger Things fans. This is why they tend not to release them too early and even throw a little misdirection out there by changing them. This happened on Stranger Things 2. The early titles released for the episodes in season two were later changed somewhat. The Duffers said this change was to stop smart alecs on Reddit from deducing too much and spoiling the surprises. The original titles were Madmax, The Boy Who Came Back to Life, The Pumpkin Patch, The Palace, The Storm, The Pollywog, The Secret Cabin, The Brain, The Lost Brother. The fact that one episode was titled The Lost Brother was because the Duffers originally conceived the character (that became) Kali as a man named Roman.

(414) Gaten Matarazzo said that his favourite Stranger Things fan theory of all is that Dustin's girlfriend Suzie is really a Soviet spy pulling all the strings from her bedroom in Salt Lake City. We can safely say though that this theory, fun though it might be, has no validity whatsoever.

(415) EarthBound, known as Mother 2 in Japan, is a 1994 Japanese role-playing video game co-developed by Ape Inc and HAL Laboratory and published by Nintendo for the Super Nintendo Entertainment System video game console. This game has been cited as a possible inspiration for Stranger Things - although the Duffers have not commonly name checked it in the way they have other games like Silent Hill and Dark Souls. EarthBound concerns a boy named Ness who learns that a universe-swallowing evil has condemned the future to eternal darkness. Ness is required to save the world and has to recruit other children to help him. One of them is a girl named Paula with psychokinetic powers. Paula has blonde hair and a pink dress. Is the makeover of Eleven in The Body a possible reference to Paula? Other similarities between Stranger Things - aside from the dark dimension angle and the psychic girl - are the small town middle America backdrop and main characters being little kids on bikes who are fighting strange and mysterious forces.

(416) The film Altered States was plainly an influence on Stranger Things. Altered States is a 1980 science fiction horror film by Ken Russell based on a novel by Paddy Chayefsky. The story is based on real life experiments by physician, neuroscientist, psychoanalyst, psychonaut, and philosopher Dr John Cunningham Lilly. Lilly invented the sensory deprivation tank. He saw the sensory deprivation tank as a means to explore the nature of human consciousness and used psychedelic drugs in his experiments. In the film, William Hurt plays a university professor who experiments with other states of consciousness by using psychotropic drugs and entering a sensory deprivation tank.

(417) The sequence in season one where the kids are on their bikes being chased by the lab's Chevy vans and Eleven makes one of the vans levitate to clear their path proved to be a tricky operation. The van was 'fired' with an air cannon but the first attempt at the stunt went wrong and destroyed some expensive camera equipment. The Duffers had to plead for permission (and money) to stage the stunt again and - thankfully - this time it went perfectly. As part of the deal for staging the stunt again the Duffers had to promise Netflix that the flying van sequence would feature in the trailer. All of this very nearly didn't happen though because the Duffers initially worried that a bike chase with kids might be too much of an obvious reference to E.T. They actually cut a lot out of the bike chase in editing because they didn't want it to feel too dragged out.

(418) When Eleven fights Henry at the lab in The Massacre at Hawkins Lab the rainbow pattern on the wall behind Henry is - appropriately enough - Upside Down.

(419) Some fans have noted the similarities between 'Hellmouths' from Buffy the Vampire Slayer and the Upside Down in Stranger Things. A Hellmouth was an area in which the barriers between dimensions was particularly weak, allowing the creation of portals between Earth and several hell dimensions. For these reasons, the Hellmouth attracts demons and other supernatural creatures, becoming a place for supernatural activity. A Hellmouth is created when a Deeper Well or Wellspring is used to cut a path to another dimension, allowing its magic to flow through.

(420) Nightmares is a largely forgotten four story horror anthology film released in 1983 and directed by Joseph Sargent. Sargent directed The Taking of Pelham One, Two Three and was a solid television director but he is most famous for Jaws: The Revenge and probably has the Razzies to prove it. Three of the segments were produced for an anthology television series called Darkroom but Universal decided to film a fourth segment and shunt them all into this theatrical feature instead. It was probably an attempt to latch onto the success of George Romero's Creepshow the previous year but Nightmares didn't do terribly well and is only really remembered today for the third story (The Bishop of Battle) where a young Emilio Estevez obsessively attempts to reach the mythical thirteenth level of a weird computer arcade game. I wonder if the arcade scenes in Stranger Things 2 might have been inspired by The Bishop of Battle?

The Bishop of Battle is a gloriously 1980s piece of nonsense. JJ Cooney (Emilio Estevez) is a video game obsessed teen with bleached hair and a Walkman the size of a brick. We meet JJ in the arcade where the graphics are predictably laughable these days and there are hustlers with headbands and fluff mustaches. JJ is very nifty at arcade games but - a cautionary tale if ever there was - his relationship to the real world and humanity is suffering as a consequence. He's flunking his grades, he barks at his mum and dad. JJ's life has become a quest that revolves around a game called The Bishop of Battle. He's heard that a boy somewhere once got to the thirteenth level, a feat generally considered to be impossible. When the kids at the arcade (including no lesser figure than Moon Unit Zappa) tire of watching him trying to beat the game and the manager pulls the plug on the machines, he is predictably crestfallen. JJ is not willing to admit defeat just yet though and sneaks out of his bedroom in the dead of night to break into the empty arcade. He's determined to get to that pesky thirteenth level but what will happen if he does? There are some enjoyably dated Tron-esque special effects in this segment that I think probably blew most of the budget for Nightmares.

The Bishop of Battle is enjoyably silly entertainment for as long as it lasts. It's fun to be in those eighties video game arcades with dated punk music blasting away when JJ goes into battle. The twist (of sorts) is relatively satisfying too.

(421) We have yet to see Steve Harrington's parents in Stranger
Things - which is an interesting piece of trivia given that we meet
the parents of most of the other characters in the show. We know
that Steve's parents must be quite rich because they have a
swimming pool and Steve drives a BMW. In season three, Steve
says that his dad refused to let him work at the family company to
'teach him a lesson'. It could be the case that Steve's parents spend a
lot of time out of Hawkins on business and leisure trips. Early on in
the show there was a weird fan theory that Steve was related to the
school bully Troy. The basis for this theory was sketchy at best.
Troy's second name is Walsh so this theory could safely be filed
among the many others which turned out to be purely speculative
and mistaken.

(422) Joe Keery's girlfriend is Maika Monroe. Maika Monroe was
the lead in the horror film It Follows in 2014. It Follows, with its
synth score, John Carpenter inspired lenses, and anachronistic small
town atmosphere, is often suggested to have been an influence on
Stranger Things. It Follows is one of the more interesting and stylish
modern horror films and certainly worth watching if you've never
seen it before.

(423) It would have cost around $4,000 to buy a Dragon's Lair
arcade machine in 1984. Adjusted for inflation that would be over
$10,000 in today's money. Don Bluth thought that Dragon's Lair
would make the traditional pixel and sprite arcade games obsolete
but he was obviously completely wrong about this. Dragon's Lair
was alluring and novel at the time but it didn't have the replayability
and enduring appeal of traditional arcade classics because it wasn't
really an arcade game to begin with.

(424) In the original plan for the show, the Duffers wanted the entire
town of Montauk to be engulfed by what would eventually become
known (in Stranger Things) as the Upside Down. A bank of mist
would swallow Montauk. Monsters would abound and the laws of
science would no longer apply. Stephen King's The Mist by way
John Carpenter's The Fog with a million other cinematic and literary
references - from Lovecraft to Close Ecounters of the Third Kind -

all colliding.

(425) The 115 year-old Lukiškes Prison in Lithuania was used as a location for Hopper's prison scenes in Stranger Things 4. This was a real prison until its closure 2019. Lukiškes Prison could hold 1,000 prisoners when it was still active. The prison had a long and dark history. It was used by Nazi Germany to house prisoners when they occupied the country during the Second World War. The facility also had a disturbing past as a prison during the Soviet Union era. The scenes in Lithuania were the first shot for season four and done in top secret.

(426) In his book The Montauk Project, Preston Nichols says that the Montauk base (known as Camp Hero) was used for a mission to the pyramids of Mars using a 'vortex' that could be walked through. No wonder hardly anyone took this book seriously! Nichols claims in his book that the big radar dish at Camp Hero was used to project an invisible beam of energy which could affect people's moods. It's probably best to approach this book as if it is a fun work of fiction. That way you might have a good time rather than nitpick everything.

(427) One of the films playing at the Starcourt Mall cinema with Back to the Future is Return to Oz. This film is an unofficial sequel to The Wizard of Oz and stars Fairuza Balk as Dorothy Gale. Return to Oz didn't do very well in 1985 and seems to have been somewhat forgotten today. The film is rather dark and scary for a supposed children's movie - which might explain why it didn't have broad appeal.

(428) Kali is the name of a Hindu goddess. Kali is one of the ten Mahavidyas, a list which combines Sakta and Buddhist goddesses.

(429) Stranger Things 4 used a third codename for one its location shoots - the name in question being Mule. Mule is a reference to the M274 Mule truck which features in the 1986 Stephen King film Maximum Overdrive (which was based on his short story Trucks). Maximum Overdrive was a critical disaster and put King off directing movies for life. There was later another adaptation of this story titled Trucks. Trucks takes place in a small desert town near Area 51. For some inexplicable reason, trucks start coming to life

and driving around of their own accord. Not only that but they seem hell bent on killing humans. A plucky band of locals end up besieged by the trucks as they try to understand what is happening. They are led by single dad Ray Porter (Timothy Busfield) and nature guide Hope Gladstone (Brenda Bakke). Let the truck dodging mayhem commence. Trucks never really justifies its own existence in a world that already has umpteen killer vehicle horror films and doesn't seem like much of an improvement on the much maligned Maximum Overdrive (which while incoherent did have a small degree of completely bonkers charm all the same). My advice would be to give Trucks a miss and watch Killdozer instead.

(430) An early fan theory was that Eleven is really Hopper's biological daughter Sarah. This theory was quite popular when people were watching season one but it seems to have a number of flaws which would be difficult to explain. Hopper seems to have no past with Terry Ives - who is clearly established by the show as Eleven's mother. If Hopper let the lab have custody of the ill Sarah to save her life, why is it that Hopper and Brenner don't seem to know each other when they meet near the end of season one? If they do know each other, why doesn't Hopper ask to see Brenner when he investigates the lab? Also, wouldn't Eleven recognise and remember Hopper if he was her real father? One other detail (for the eagle eyed) is that Sarah and Eleven have different eye colours.

(431) An occupational hazard for the cast on Stranger Things is that they can easily end up losing their voices due to all the screaming they have do. This has happened to Noah Schnapp, Dacre Montgomery, and Millie Bobby Brown at various points on the show. Losing your voice is obviously not ideal for an actor because you do actually need to be able to speak to perform your job! Millie Bobby Brown said that Shawn Levy came up with a clever solution to this problem when they were shooting Stranger Things 3. He told her to save the really big screams for the last takes before she was due a day or two off. This seemed to do the trick. If you appear in a horror production which requires you to shout and scream a lot you have to learn how to 'manage' your voice so you'll get through it without going too hoarse.

(432) In the season three episode The Mall Rats, a phone book gives

numbers in the 765 area code. This was not actually the case until 1997. In 1985 it would have been area code 317 in Indiana.

(433) It took trials with fifteen hair care products before they found the right one to use on Joe Keery for Steve's hair. Keery, contrary to rumour, is not banned from cutting his hair by Netflix. If he did have his hair chopped off for another part they would presumably give him a hairpiece in Stranger Things.

(434) Ham radio is still used by some two million licensed operators all over the world. Though seen as an old-fashioned form of communication it can still play an important role in a crisis. Whenever they depict a survivalist type character in an end of the world film they are usually operating a ham radio.

(435) The shotgun Nancy uses to blast Vecna is a Winchester Model 1200. Nancy saws the barrels off after Jason Carver tells her that in close quarter combat someone would just grab the gun and take it off her. Sawing the barrels off in reality would make it lesss effective. Gun experts say that Jason's claim that this weapon is not much use for anything other than killing small birds is not true at all.

(436) The eagle-eyed will notice that Eleven wears a ring in Stranger Things 4. This was presumably a gift from Mike when she left Hawkins at the end of season three.

(437) David Harbour said he was a bit creeped out by the Demogorgon suit when he first encountered it on the set in season one. It was the freakishly long arms which he found the most disconcerting. Demogorgons don't seem to have eyes so we must presume they maybe have heightened senses and use sounds and vibrations to hunt.

(438) Lucas wears the number 8 basketball shirt in season four in tribute to the late Kobe Bryant.

(439) The funfair in Stranger Things 3 features the Gravitron - a ride created in 1983. This ride is completely enclosed, with 48 padded panels lining the inside wall. Riders lean against these panels, which are angled back. As the ride rotates, centrifugal force is exerted

against the pads by the rider, removing the rider from the floor, due to the slant. The ride can reach a maximum speed of 24 rpm in less than 20 seconds. The Gravitron is something of an acquired taste and has been known to make people vomit.

(440) This sequence where Eleven takes out Brenner's agents in spectacular (if grisly) fashion in the season one finale is the most obvious example of the influence on Eleven of the character of Lucy from the manga Elfin Lied. Both Lucy and Eleven escape from a laboratory and have amazing powers. The main difference is the use of violence. Lucy is known for gruesome blood soaked kills. Eleven in Stranger Things is not so ferocious or cold blooded and Stranger Things - naturally - is not as violent or gore caked as a Japanese manga. The school corridor scene is a rare case though of Eleven at her most extreme. She is willing to do anything to escape. It is the closest we get to manga Eleven.

(441) Note in Stranger Things 4 how Robin appears to have only told Steve that she is gay. In the small town Hawkins of 1986 it is clearly still a lot more difficult to be openly gay than it is today.

(442) You can see a Time-Out arcade in Stranger Things 3. Time-Out Amusement Centers were a chain of arcades located in malls across America. The first one opened in 1970. The popularity of arcades began to dwindle in the 1990s. The obvious factor in this was that the video games you could play at home were rapidly getting better and better and giving you an arcade experience from the comfort of your bedroom (where you also didn't need to have a bag of coins in order to play). If you could play games like Doom, Screamer and Quake at home why would you need to go to an arcade anymore?

Shopping malls eventually began to sell their arcade machines because they were no longer profitable and the demise of the video game arcade began. As a reaction to the revolution and quantum leap in home gaming, arcades introduced motion simulator arcade machines like Typhoon where you would be thrown around in the seat as you played the game. This was an attempt to make arcade games unique again but this sort of thing never really caught on enough to turn in a tidy profit and save arcades. Arcades today are more of a nostalgia thing than a necessity. If you can play games like Doom Eternal at home it's hard to see what they could do in an arcade machine to really knock your socks off.

(443) When Pac-Man was first launched in Japan in 1980 it was something of a flop. It was the popularity of the game in the United States that made it so famous. The Duffer Brothers and Sadie Sink said that Pac-Man was the game they played the most between takes on the Palace Arcade set when they were shooting Stranger Things 2. Hasbro released a Stranger Things Palace Arcade Handheld Electronic Game. The device allows you to play twenty vintage games which include Pac-Man, Dig Dug, Galaga, and Galaxian.

(444) At the end of season four, Lucas is reading the Stephen King/Peter Straub book The Talisman to Max at the hospital. This book is about a boy who must access a parallel world to save his mother. For many years the rights were held by Steven Spielberg but he never got around to adapting the book. It was recently announced that the Duffer Brothers will adapt the book in a TV show. The Talisman is the last major work by Stephen King in the 1980s yet to be adapted. The fact that Steven Spielberg planned to adapt it has a perfect symmetry as a Duffer Brothers project because, as any Stranger Things will know, the original pitch for Stranger Things was to make a show that felt like a Stephen King book directed by Steven Spielberg.

(445) One can see many cinematic influences in the Pennhurst and lab scenes in season four besides Silence of the Lambs. Martin Scorsese's Shutter Island, One Flew Over the Cuckoo's Nest (which is surely the most famous psychiatric ward film ever made), Terry Gilliam's 12 Monkeys, and M. Night Shyamalan's 2019 film Glass (which takes place at Raven Hill Memorial psychiatric hospital - the Duffers are well aware of Shyamalan after working for him on Wayward Pines). Other influences include the excellent 1995 Lovecraft inspired John Carpenter film In the Mouth of Madness, the interesting and finely acted horror sequel The Exorcist III (which mostly takes place in a psychiatric ward), and the original 1988 Child's Play (which is about the murderous possessed toy doll Chucky and has psychiatric hospital scenes). Hellbound: Hellraiser II, which mostly takes place in a psychiatric hospital and is a fairly

solid sequel, was also a very obvious influence on Stranger Things 4.

(446) The character of Argyle (who takes his name from the limo driver in Die Hard) is partly inspired by Sean Penn's Jeff Spicoli in Fast Times at Ridgemont High.

(447) The disturbing sketches of the Flayer that Will Byers draws in Stranger Things 2 (which eventually cover most of the Byers) house were mostly done by scenic artists but Noah Schnapp personally contributed many himself. Noah did some research about possessed people to prepare for season two. Season two was by far, at the time of writing, the meatiest season for Noah Schnapp as he was allocated 115 more lines than he enjoyed in season one (Will Byers was unavoidably largely offscreen in season one what with him being trapped in the Upside Down for most of it) and his character Will Byers was a pivotal part of the plot. That was not the case with seasons three and four though - where Noah Schnapp was often sidelined and the Duffers didn't seem to find too much for Will Byers to do.

(448) Winona Ryder said she is very thankful for Stranger Things because it came along at a time when she wasn't getting many offers and felt like her career had gone a bit flat. "I've been really blessed and lucky to have the career I've had but this show has really changed my life. It came at a time when there wasn't a lot going on for me and women my age, and it's opened a lot of opportunities up. It's just been an absolute joy to work on something for this long with people that you love, and watching these amazing kids grow up."

(449) Dacre Montgomery wore his own Saint Christopher necklace while playing Billy Hargrove in Stranger Things. Dacre said that on his last day of shooting he stole one of Billy's tank tops to take home with him. There would appear to be a costume easter egg at the end of season three in that Billy is dressed like Jack Burton in Big Trouble in Little China.

(450) Night of the Creeps is a cult 1986 low-budget sci-fi horror film written and directed by Fred Dekker. Dekker must feature on any list of the unluckiest people in Hollywood. After Night of the Creeps and his affectionate horror spoof The Monster Squad he seemed to

have a great future but the Robocop 3 debacle made him persona non
grata and he was banished to television script editing. A shame
really. Night of the Creeps throws in every B-film horror/science
fiction reference imaginable and like many eighties horror films has
its tongue planted in cheek, riffing as it does on 1950s paranoia sci-fi
and the conventions of the eighties college campus comedy film.
What are the connections that bind Night of the Creeps with Stranger
Things? There are quite a few. The teen hero is something of an
outcast (not unlike Jonathan) who has feelings for a girl with a
popular 'cool' jock bouffant haired sunglasses loving boyfriend (not
unlike his namesake - first season Stranger Things Steve). One might
say too that Hopper is a rather gruff Tom Atkins sort of hero hero.
The plucky teenagers must also fight unfathomable monsters just
like the teenagers in Stranger Things and - once again - there is
secret lab intrigue. And most interesting of all is the slug that Will
coughs up in the first season finale of Stranger Things. It would not
come as a tremendous surprise if this was inspired by Night of the
Creeps.

(451) December saw the first inkling of what was set to be a deluge
of Stranger Things 4 merch when Walmart released a retro Stranger
Things cassette player. The player came with a cassette which
Walmart, on their promos, said would contain a secret message
about season four. Those who purchased the player and listened to
the message were rather disappointed though that it didn't amount to
anything tremendously illuminating. At least they still had a
collector's item piece of merch in the cassette player.
The message heard on the cassette was as follows - "Hello, this is
Yuri of Yuri's Fish and Fly. Would you like to book a trip with me
and perhaps together we soar the Arctic and fish with the polar
bears? I'm sorry, are you speaking? I cannot hear you because this is
a pre-recorded message, you peanut brain. I got you, I got you good.
I must be very busy now, perhaps with a customer, perhaps with my
beautiful Katinka, but I'm pleased to book a trip for you at other
time for a good, fair price. Much more fair price than Jerry's Arctic
Boat Charters. Just leave a number and I will call you when less
busy."

(452) There is, perhaps in tribute to Max, a copy of the film Valley
Girl in the Family Video store in season three. This romantic

comedy supplied an early role for Nicholas Cage. Valley Girl is a term used to describe the stereotype of an air-headed young woman (most likely from California) only interested in material things. The term was popularised when it was the title of a 1982 Frank Zappa single. By the way, Sadie Sink said she found it quite amusing that she was cast as a character from California in Stranger Things because in reality she is very pale-skinned and hates the sun.

(453) In the original plan for Stranger Things, Jonathan Byers was supposed to work in the Hawkins cinema. There was going to be a sequence where Jonathan and Nancy took refuge in the cinema to hide from the stalking Demogorgon. These plans were all changed - although there is still a cinema in Hawkins (which we only ever seem to see from the outside). The building used for the Hawkins cinema is actually a furniture store in Jackson. What they do is just disguise the front of the store to make it look like the exterior of a picture house.

(454) John Carpenter's The Fog is set in a small picturesque fishing town called Antonio Bay. It's almost one hundred years since a ship was wrecked on the rocks in heavy fog there and - as old sea dog Machen (John Houseman) tells some terrified children over a beachside campfire in the prologue - should the fog ever return, legend has it the victims of this shipwreck will return too to extract a bloody revenge for their premature departure from this world. As the town prepares to celebrate its centenary, the fog inexorably drifts in to mark its return to Antonio Bay. Stranger Things borrows not only a brooding sense of atmosphere from The Fog but also a key device where a DJ (Adrienne Barbeau) finds that her broadcasts can intercept something very spooky and netherworld. Stranger Things does a similar thing with the school's ham radio acting as a medium to contact another dimension.

(455) The Duffers have studiously avoided becoming involved in any side projects during the duration of Stranger Things because they have always found it difficult to concentrate on more than one thing at a time. As long as Stranger Things is still going the Duffers want to give the show their 100% undivided attention. They had no desire to do anything else. The laser guided focus of the Duffers to concentrate on Stranger Things and Stranger Things ALONE was

one of the many reasons why the show was so well crafted and maintained such high standards.

(456) The Duffer Brothers and David Harbour later confessed that they didn't fool anyone when they pretended to be unsure about whether or not Hopper was really dead after Stranger Things 3. No one actually believed that David Harbour wasn't coming back to the show. This attempted ruse had some similarities with season two where they tried to be ambiguous about whether or not Millie Bobby Brown and Eleven were going to be back (Eleven was of course vapourised into a cloud of dust after fighting the Demogorgon the last time we saw her in season one). No one really bought this intrigue either. It would have been astonishing if Eleven hadn't come back for season two given that Brown was the breakout star of season one - and so it proved in the end when Eleven was very much a part of Stranger Things 2.

(457) The underrated 1988 remake of The Blob has a number of uncanny similarities with Stranger Things 3. It has a small town atmosphere, a sheriff, and some horror scenes in a hospital. The home of the heroine Shawnee Smith in The Blob also looks a lot like the Wheeler house inside and the hero Kevin Dillon has an outrageous mullet like Billy Hargrove. The Blob remake also naturally has mysterious government scientists in hazmat suits. It even has kids being smuggled into a cinema to watch a horror film and then the movie cutting out because of an inexplicable event. The military scientists in The Blob want to get hold of the organism to use as a biological weapon. This is sort of what the Soviets are trying to do in Stranger Things 3. Given all the similarities, you would be amazed if the Duffers had never watched The Blob remake.

(458) Cinematographer Lachlan Milne said the scene in Stranger Things 3 where Eleven and Max are looking at a family portrait on the wall (and their faces are reflected back through the portrait) was complex to shoot. "This shot was actually in the script, so it's straight from the Duffer Brothers. Millie Bobby Brown had just returned back to work after fracturing her knee during a break in shooting so she couldn't move too freely but was a trooper for soldiering on through it as best she could. You have to over light the people in the reflection in a way that if you were to pan over to them

they would be a stop or two overexposed, but it looks normal in the glass. It was a tight spot and being a real location we couldn't pull walls, but we found a way."

(459) When Sullivan and the military storm the missile silo in Papa this is a homage to the corridor sequence at the start of the original Star Wars. Sullivan's obsession with Eleven is somewhat on the vague side in season four in terms of his motivation but we do see that he seems to connect the deaths in Hawkins (at the hands of Vecna) with the gruesome deaths of Connie Frazier and the government agents in the school corridor (which happened in the season one finale). Sullivan therefore seems to believe that Eleven ALONE is responsible for all of these strange and harrowing deaths.

(460) Fan theories in the past have included the suggestions that the Mind Flayer is really an evil Upside Down version of Barb and the Demogorgon is Will Byers from the future.

The first theory went like this - What if Barb somehow mutated in the Upside Down and collected all the negative energy present in the environment and herself (for surely poor Barb would have a lot to be angry about) and this all manifested itself in Barb becoming an all powerful entity in the Upside Down? Though fun, this theory obviously had no basis in fact. Another early theory on a similar theme suggested that the Mind Flayer could be Hopper's daughter Sarah. What if she became trapped in the Upside Down and over the years morphed into the Mind Flayer? The Will Byers theory was proposed by a fan on reddit, who wrote - 'So this is pure fan speculation but I'm in the middle of re-watching Stranger Things and thought I'd post my ideas here. I'm not sure if this idea has been floated around but after watching and then looking up other theories I started thinking about this.

The Demagorgon is a grown up Will Byers fully transformed by The Mind Flayer with the sole purpose of taking over and repopulating on other worlds/universes. I'll start out with what we know from the show. In season 1 we're told The Upside Down is a dimension out of space and time that the government tears a gateway into with all their experimentation. So what if The Upside Down isn't just a parallel dimension, but more of a parallel universe. They said themselves it's a place outside of regular space-time, so maybe it's possible that The Upside Down is actually Hawkins in the future. Why else would there be buildings and other structures there? Who built them? It works like this: the government experiments happen, a gateway is created using Eleven. The Demagorgon is loose in our world where it starts to kill/find hosts for its babies. Eventually the Mind Flayer is able to "terraform" that world, and waits for the next parallel universe gateway to be opened by the government in a loop. That's why the Demagorgon in season one knew exactly where to find Will, and also didn't kill him immediately. And also why Will was the only person who was snatched that wasn't actually bleeding. Notice at the end of season one we see Barb's corpse among a few other skeletons. Not only that, but it sticks almost entirely to the Byers' house as if it's looking for something. Nancy and Jonathan manage to pinpoint its main hunting grounds, which included the Byers' house. Nobody else reported weird stuff in their walls, so why would it be so adamant on staying to that area?

In season two Will also specifically says The Mind Flayer doesn't want to kill him, but everyone else. Maybe because it always needs Will as the catalyst to actually take over? Could also explain why it tries to take over Billy later-this universe succeeds in "exorcising" Will before he can fully transform. It also could explain why the Demagorgon is humanoid in shape. There are obviously flaws, one of the main ones being: if the Mind Flayer works in an endless loop of multiverse takeover, how did it first start? What do you guys think? Please tell me if I've gotten anything wrong in the canon or anything. I'll also add that in season two when Will gets infected by The Mind Flayer, he describes his visions as "memories" but not specifically his. And he also says that it feels like they're all happening at the same time. Could they be Will's collective memories from other universes where the same thing is happening?'

(461) A John Carpenter film that may be an influence on Stranger Things is 1987's Prince of Darkness. The influence of Halloween, The Fog and The Thing on Stranger Things is more obvious so let's discuss the less obvious Prince of Darkness. A Catholic priest (Donald Pleasence) asks a group of young post-graduate physicist students led by Professor Howard Birack (Victor Wong) to investigate something very strange in a derelict Los Angeles church.

The priest's worries concern a swirling, pulsating green liquid contained in an ornate cannister in the basement where it has been hidden away from the world for centuries. One of John Carpenter's more incoherent eighties offerings, Prince of Darkness is a film that is somehow less than the sum of its parts and sees the director once again paying homage to British writer Nigel Kneale - who was famous for his frequent fusion of science and the supernatural. This is something that Stranger Things also does quite frequently. Prince of Darkness is fun but suffers slightly from some lackadaisical pacing and seems to throw too many ideas into the mix without them ever completely meshing into a satisfying whole. Still, there are some interesting components here that make one think of Stranger Things. The scientific trappings, the alternate dimension/mirror shenanigans, and that famous and unmistakable Carpenter music.

(462) It is possible that Lucas Sinclair got his first name from the cult eighties teen film 'Lucas' starring Corey Haim. Lucas marked the film debut of Winona Ryder. Many believe though the name Lucas is a nod to George Lucas.

(463) The games Dragon's Lair and Dig-dug were chosen in Stranger Things 2 to forshadow plot events according to the Duffers "We were hoping to do with the arcade what we did in season one with D&D, which was to do a bit of foreshadowing for the whole season, with Lucas getting Princess Daphne, and the monsters in Dig-Dug. We were hoping to roughly set up where we were going to go in the next nine hours." The Duffers both say that they actually dislike Dragon's Lair as a game (and they aren't huge fans of Dig Dug either by all accounts). "Dragon's Lair we played a lot as kids. It's a fun game to look at — it's not a very fun game to play. Everyone who played it as a kid had the same experience: It's outrageously expensive, it looks really cool, it draws you in like a magnet, and then it just takes your money and is very frustrating. All these barcades are popping up now, and I was at one recently and they had Dragon's Lair there. And no one is playing it because it's not a very good game. But it's still 50 cents! It's 2017 now, and 50 cents is a lot less, but it still felt like it was ripping you off. It's such an impossible game."

(464) Millie Bobby Brown was delighted that Eleven was adopted

by Joyce Byers at the end of Stranger Things 3 because it meant she finally got some scenes with Noah Schnapp. Millie and Noah are best friends in real life but their characters barely say a word to each other in the first three seasons of the show. While the characters of Eleven and Will Byers are not exactly chatterboxes and don't have long endless conversations in season four at the very least we do actually see them together for a change.

(465) In season four, Jonathan, Mike, Will, and Argyle are sort of in WarGames by way of National Lampoon's Vacation. Their arc often feels like Amblin mashed up with Harold & Kumar. This was designed to be a contrast with the classic horror riffs in Hawkins and Hopper's prison drama - which eventually morphs into science fiction and horror.

The Island of Doctor Moreau was one of the many influences on the Hopper arc in Stranger Things 4. The Island of Doctor Moreau is a quasi-allegorical science fiction novel published in 1896. The story concerns the frequently terrified Edward Prendick, a shipwrecked sailor who is rescued in the South Seas and ends up on a remote and mysterious island where a hubristic scientist named Moreau is conducting all manner of strange and troubling experiments. Prendick is soon spooked by the strange sights he catches glimpses of in the jungle and the cries he hears late at night from his room and becomes very curious to find out what exactly is going on as this unsettling tale unfolds and the macabre secrets of Moreau are gradually revealed.

(466) The shed where Will Byers is trapped by the Demogorgon in the ever first episode has an upside down horseshoe above the door. This is a symbol of bad luck. It's safe to say that the curse of the horseshoe struck true and Will had wretched luck for two solid seasons.

(467) One Stephen King story that is never connected to Stranger Things is The Langoliers. But, with some leaps of logic and a large helping of speculation, maybe it could be. The story has a small group of passengers waking up on a plane and discovering that everyone else on the plane has vanished. They land the plane - thanks to an airline pilot passenger - at a small airport in Maine but

bizarre events puzzle them when they arrive. Matches do not light, food and drink tastes off or flat, the sun goes up and down too quickly, and sound does not echo. What on earth is going on? The world the characters find themselves trapped in with The Langoliers is sort of like the Upside Down in that it is a mirror of our world but a dark mirror. The story uses concepts like time travel travel and other dimensions and there are mysterious creatures who are - quite literally - consuming the present all around them. Maybe there could be some parallels in that the creatures in Stranger Things seem to be intent of 'consuming' dimensions.

(468) The eerie chime of a grandfather clock which heralds Vecna's arrival was also used in season one for the arrival of the Demogorgon. The production team said that they purchased four vintage grandfather clocks to use in Stranger Things 4.

(469) In the season four sequences where we are in Vecna's hellish red mindscape, the plan was to show that Flayer particles were responsible for holding up all the boulders and objects floating in the air. In the end though they simply didn't have the time to add in all these digital special effects.

(470) A lot of fans assumed that Mason Dye was doing a Tom Cruise impersonation as Jason Carver in Stranger Things 4 but that's actually his real voice. Jason's hairstyle does seem to be Tom Cruise inspired though.

(471) The white vest Murray wears in the season three finale is another comic nod to Bruce Willis in Die Hard.

(472) Mayor Kline is dressed like Gordon Gekko from Oliver Stone's Wall Street in Stranger Things 3. Gekko is a ruthless corporate raider on Wall Street fond of braces and expensive shirts. The greedy and crooked Kline would probably admire a dodgy character like Gekko.

(473) Noah Schnapp later confessed that he didn't have a clue who Winona Ryder was before he was cast in Stranger Things as her character's son. He'd never seen any of her films. To be fair to Noah he was only about eleven when he was cast in Stranger Things.

(474) The Duffers said the original plan with season one of Stranger Things was to only use practical special effects in homage to the 1980s but this proved completely impossible in the end.

(475) The red vines in Stranger Things 2 from the Upside Down rather evoke the red 'Martian weed' in HG Wells' The War of the Worlds. 'Apparently the vegetable kingdom in Mars, instead of having green for a dominant colour, is of a vivid blood-red tint. At any rate, the seeds which the Martians (intentionally or accidentally) brought with them gave rise in all cases to red-coloured growths. Only that known popularly as the red weed, however, gained any footing in competition with terrestrial forms. The red creeper was quite a transitory growth, and few people have seen it growing. For a time, however, the red weed grew with astonishing vigour and luxuriance.' The parallel between Imperialism and the European colonisation of indigenous peoples and the vicious and merciless Martian assault seems far from accidental in Wells' book.

Given the treatment of less developed nations around the world and man's cruelty to many species of animals, the author suggests we are simply receiving a dose of our own medicine. 'Are we such apostles of mercy as to complain if the Martians warred in the same spirit?' There is a deep paranoia too perhaps in the novel. A fear of being invaded one day by a ruthless foreign power. If Stranger Things 2 has a subtext beneath the simple horror sci-fi fun, this subtext is similar to the one in The War of the Worlds. Fear of others. Invaders. Terrorists. As Dustin will later say of the Mind Flayer - "It views other races like us as inferior to itself. It wants to spread and take over other dimensions." If we really looked hard enough perhaps we could see a connection between the inhabitants of the Upside Down and the residents of Hawkins with Wells' The Time Machine. The beautiful, childlike and thoughtless Eloi living out an idle, vacuous existence on the surface while the subterranean troglodytic Morlocks lurk underground and prey on the Eloi when night falls.

(476) The term "Slurpee" came from the audio slurping sound this beverage makes when it is slurped through a straw. A man named Omar Knedlik is the person who apparently invented this ice theme drink - though it was an accient rather than something he came up

with. When his soda fountain broke down, Knedlik put some soda in
the freezer to keep it cool but he left some of it in there too long and
it stated to ice up. And so was born the slurpee. The references to
'Slurpees' in Stranger Things 3 may well come from the cult Winona
Ryder film Heathers. In that movie Winona Ryder's character was
fond of cherry Slurpees.

(477) 'Mouthbreather' - a term Eleven and the boys use in season one
of Stranger Things - is slang for a stupid person or annoying person.
If someone was getting on your nerves you might say - 'You are
SUCH a mouthbreather'.

(478) The short wig that Millie Bobby Brown wears in season four
was a long wig cut down by the hairdressing department. Due to
child labour laws, the hairdressing department had to learn how to
apply the wig in no more than 35 minutes.

(479) The hairdressing department said it was novel and very
enjoyable to do the 1950s scenes in Stranger Things 4 because it was
a rare chance for them to do something other than 1980s hairstyles.

(480) Eleven has a Bambi figurine on her desk in Stranger Things 4.
This is a symbol of how vulnerable feels without her powers and
how alone she feels without Hopper and cut adrift from her friends
in Hawkins.

(481) Eleven's return at the end of The Mind Flayer, where you only
see a slow motion shot of her footwear entering the cabin at first,
was a homage to a scene of Neo entering a building in The Matrix.

(482) The Police song Every Breath You Take closes Stranger
Things 2 as the Flayer ominously lurks beyond our dimension and
the Snow Ball dance. In the original script for this episode it was
planned to close the episode with the Phil Collins song In the Air
Tonight.

(483) When they were shooting the season four finale The
Piggyback, Joe Keery mistimed a swing with an axe in a Steve
Harrington scene and damaged an expensive camera.

(484) Erica seems very keen to get her hands on a copy of Duck Hunt in Stranger Things 4. Duck Hunt is a 1984 light gun shooter video game developed and published by Nintendo for the Nintendo Entertainment System (NES) video game console and the Nintendo Vs. System arcade hardware. The game was released in 1984.

(485) One of the inspirations for the Pennhurst Hospital scenes in Stranger Things 4 was the 1999 Winona Ryder film Girl, Interrupted. From 1967, eighteen-year-old Susanna Kaysen spent two years at the famous McLean Hospital (of Sylvia Plath fame) in a psychiatric ward for teenage girls after a short session with a psychiatrist she'd never seen before. Girl, Interrupted was a memoir of her time there and told in a series of short non-chronological vignettes in which we, and Kaysen, slowly try and piece together the events that led to her spending so long at McLean and get a portrait of life in this strange and sometimes disturbing environment. An adaptation of Girl, Interrupted was a dream project for Ryder and she played Kaysen in the movie and also produced the film. Girl, Interrupted is generally held up as the film which propelled Angelina Jolie to stardom. Se got an Oscar for her supporting role as the free-spirited Lisa. Lisa is the most vivid of the people Kaysen met in the hospital and features in the memoir quite a lot. You'd probably have to say (with apologies to Winona Ryder) that the book is much better than the film. The memoir is always fascinating for the glimpse it affords us into this strange secret world and is often a very poignant book as we read about these troubled souls. Although disturbing at times, Girl, Interrupted is an eloquent and very personal memoir.

(486) A walkie-talkie (more formally known as a handheld transceiver, or HT) is a hand-held, portable, two-way radio transceiver. Its development during the Second World War has been variously credited to Donald L Hings, radio engineer Alfred J Gross, and engineering teams at Motorola. First used for infantry, similar designs were created for field artillery and tank units, and after the war, walkie-talkies spread to public safety and eventually commercial use. The boys in Stranger Things use walkie-talkies a lot.

(487) Another film the Stranger Things costume designers used as inspiration for the fashion of the teenagers in the show was Tuff

Turf. Tuff Turf is a 1985 American drama film directed by Fritz Kiersch and starring James Spader and Kim Richards. A young Robert Downey Jr. was also in this movie.

(488) Charlotte and Clara Ward are the twins who played the baby Eleven in the season two flashbacks set in the lab of Dr Brenner. Like the Price twins (who play Holly Wheeler in Stranger Things), Charlotte and Clara have also played Judith Grimes in The Walking Dead. So if you add Martie Blair and Millie Bobby Brown, four people have now portrayed Eleven in the show.

(489) It is estimated that Eleven kills (appropriately enough) eleven people in the first season of Stranger Things. Her victims are all lab workers or government agents.

(490) Eleven kills an estimated two people in Stranger Things 4 - the pilot and gunner of the helicopter trying to kill her in Papa. One could add Henry Creel too if we count the 1979 flashbacks. Eleven is sometimes assumed to have killed three orderlies when her powers briefly return in The Nina Project. One assumes that they could have survived though - albeit with plenty of bruises for their trouble.

(491) Eleven kills four people in Stranger Things 3. These were Russian baddies at the mall. Eleven threw a car at them to save her friends!

(492) Scientist Marius Stan said the further dimensions might possibly exist and scientific experiments on the subject are ongoing. "They are smashing particles against each other at very high energy. They hope to create mini black holes with very high density of matter — even light can't get out of that. By doing that, they want to prove theories that say our universe is, in fact multidimensional, has more than three or four dimensions we are used to."

(493) Eleven doesn't seem to kill anyone in Stranger Things 2 - which is a rare occurrence in the show.

(494) The moment where Lucas shoots the Demogorgon in the season one finale with his wrist-rocket and it is thrown back (we quickly deduce that Eleven REALLY did this - not Lucas) is a riff

on the scene in Saving Private Ryan where Tom Hanks fires a futile shot at a tank just as the tank is about to be bombed by an aircraft. You might say then that in this instance Lucas was the distraction and Eleven was the heavy artillery.

(495) The Duffer Brothers said they wanted the horror in Stranger Things to be rooted in science - specifically science that is out of control. They personally find the concept of 'dark science' things like alternate dimensions and aliens (though aliens obviously don't feature in Stranger Things) to be scarier than gosts and the supernatural.

(496) The budget for season one of Stranger Things was set at $6 million an episode - which was not exactly chicken feed but fairly modest by Hollywood standards. The entire budget on season one would only cover the budget for one and a half episodes in season four. This illustrates how the scope of Stranger Things has increased since it began.

(497) The DemoDogs kill over 40 people in Stranger Things 2.

(498) The entire Snow Ball sequence in the season two finale took two days to shoot. The child extras were originally told they were being hired for a (obviously fictitious) show called Wonder View. They must have been very excited when they learned they were actually going to be in Stranger Things.

(499) After season two there was a fan theory that Erica Sinclair had some connection to the Hawkins Lab. This theory stemmed from the fact that Erica had crayon drawings of rainbows and sunflowers in her room. The comatose Terry Ives can only say the words "Breathe. Sunflower. Three to the right, four to the left. 450. Rainbow. Breathe. Sunflower." after her electro shock treatment in the lab when she tried to get her daughter (Eleven/Jane) back. It seems this connection was merely a little mischief Easter egg by the production staff that didn't really mean anything.

(500) Dr Brenner refers to the Hawkins Lab as a 'hospital' in season four - which is an interesting choice of words. In a season one flashback where Hopper's daughter is in hospital we see Hopper on

the same lab stairs that he later finds the injured Dr Owens siting on in the season two finale. This suggests Sarah was treated at the Hawkins Lab. The wider significance of these apparent connections, should any be intended, has yet to be explained.

REFERENCES

Upside Down: The Unofficial and Unauthorised Stranger Things Companion by James Forster (Telos Publishing)

1000 Facts About Stranger Things by Nick Bryce

https://www.reddit.com/r/FanTheories/

https://www.imdb.com